The Bitter Pill of Truth:
A Cure for Judeo-Christianity

By J.M. Ladd
©2008

"It is the responsibility of the intellectuals to speak the truth and expose the lies."
Noam Chomsky, 1928 –

"On religion in particular, the time appears to me to have come, when it is a duty of all who, being qualified in point of knowledge, have, on mature consideration, satisfied themselves that the current opinions are not only false, but hurtful, to make their dissent known."
John Stuart Mill, 1806 - 1873

One: The preface I originally did not want to write

I would like to begin this book by asking you the reader a question: why have you chosen to read this book? Are you a non-believer, a person without religion that would like to re-confirm as to why you feel and believe the way you do? Are you a person who is conflicted with your own faith, and are seeking to either confirm it or have reasons for abandoning it? Are you a person of faith whose convictions and beliefs are strong and you are just interested in seeing what sort of "trash" us non-faithful can dish up? For whatever reason you have picked up this book I would like to thank you, and hope that you finish it and come away with something positive. While I understand that much of this book will be negative, and much of what will be brought to light somewhat distasteful if you are weak in your faith or are unused to having it dissected and exposed, I hope that all who read it can glean something useful and helpful. Raise your consciousness, open your mind, and try to see things without the God-colored glasses that far too many people wear.

While much of these thoughts in this book are my own, I am quite sure that many more are age-old arguments, posed by minds much sharper and more knowledgeable than my own. Some I have re-worded, re-tooled, and re-vamped. Why? Because not everyone has read every book, and not everyone has heard the full breadth of arguments for a humanistic, *sans theistic* lifestyle. If I happen to step on any toes in this book, please forgive and indulge me. There is so much credit to give, especially to people like Dennett, Dawkins, Hitchens, Paine, Barker, Sagan, Hawkins, Einstein, and even to modern, every-day bloggers, so I hope these people take this work as a pat on their own backs.

I have decided to fill this book with quotes by famous people that have lived throughout the ages. I hope their words inspire you not only to open and free your mind, but to research them and their ideals. Aside from that, I have chosen not to have any footnotes, a bibliography, or anything of the like. The reason for this is that the information in this book is not top-secret. It is not hidden away in arcane tombs, ancient libraries, or not for the layperson to discover. It is astounding the sheer volume of facts and lessons one can learn simply by being educated about history, the world in which we live, and having the ability to truly see the forest through the trees.

If you have come for the truth, I am glad to present it to you in a frank and journalistic way with some humor mixed in. I must warn you though; the truth is a bitter pill and it can be hard to swallow. It is always said that the truth hurts, but it is not my intention to hurt you, but rather to open your eyes to just what forces keep us humans bound to religions that are, at their base level, harmful to a decent, positive, and peaceful society. I would also like to expose the lies and deceptions of religion, the ways in which it has hurt and hindered humankind, and show that a person does not need ancient and outdated texts and ceremonial self-debasement to be decent, loving, caring, compassionate, and moral.

If you are wondering what my credentials are for writing this book, I will gladly present them to you now. I am an educated human being. That alone is enough, or should be. It does not matter which religion (if any) with which I was raised. I grew out of religion naturally at an early age. It is important to know that while I was raised in a home that had religion, it was not mandatory, not shoved down my or my siblings' throats, and was not key to every-day life. I was not abused, not molested, not ignored. I had, in fact, a wonderful childhood and am lucky enough to have been raised by loving, caring, and giving parents. I had and have decent friends, do not drink or do drugs, and had no emotional trauma while growing up. In essence, there are no emotional, physical, or spiritual hang-ups that have shaped my religious views. I am simply an educated and tolerant person who has studied many religions, and knows history. It is not that I "hate" God, for one cannot hate an imaginary thing. I hate what is done in God's name, or how God is used as an excuse and a means to an end.

The onus to disprove God, or any supreme being, is not upon the non-believer. The faithful have the burden, rather, of proving that their deity exists, and that their faith is the "true" way. So far there has been insufficient proof to anything of the sort, especially any deity representing love, kindness, tolerance, benevolence, and peace. Irrationality, impatience, intolerance, and emotionally instability are not qualities I would seek in my chosen deity, and so I reject the idea of the god of Judeo-Christianity. As a realist and a humanist, I do not need the web of religion to hold me fast, nor do I need it as a crutch. I do not even need it as a strengthening agent, for I am strong and whole on my own without the need of supernatural backup.

I am not an atheist, but an anti-theist. My belief is that humankind is only bogged down by religion, and that humans do not need dogma and religions to dictate what "moral" behavior is. Before man invented religion, long after each individual belief system succumbs to modern-day sensibilities and rationality, and notwithstanding religion's power, men and women would have come to the same moral conclusions had not a single religion been created. It is wrong to kill one another. It is wrong for children to be harmed in any way. It is wrong to cannibalize each other, it is wrong to steal, to torture, to rape, to enslave, to deceive and so on, yet these things still take place by the religious and the non-religious alike, and all of the afore-mentioned horrors are widely found in the bible's parables and teachings. Of all religions and the gods they tout (or have touted) none has yet to stop any of this behavior, and, in fact, religion has been the main cause of many of these crimes. Values and morals come from living together; from the force we call human conscience and human consciousness. We had values and morals long before any religion, and there are not many religions still being practiced, or that have faded away as time progresses that has done a single thing to forward and evolve human morals.

While reading this book, please keep in mind that when I mention God (with a capital G) or religion that I am referring specifically to the god of Judaism and/or Christianity and these two religions unless I state otherwise. I say 'and/or' because some people do believe that the God of Judaism and the God of Christianity are different gods, while the majority believes He/She/It is one in the same.

I will use the word 'fear' much throughout this book, and it is because I have found that it is fear that is the glue of Judeo-Christianity. The only real example I would need to cite is the word that so many traditional and fundamental Christians use: *God-fearing.* I always found that word a hindrance to the religions, as any deity that one needs to fear is not one worth of much respect or adoration. Just like the bully who takes your lunch money is not so much respected as he is feared, so any deity that would force you to pay homage and give constant praise via fear mongering dogma and threats of severe, ever-lasting bodily harm falls into the same category. Without fear, Judeo-Christianity collapses in upon itself. I will also apologize now for I can be quite redundant at times, but I do try and get my points across, so please bear with me.

Although so many millions of people will say they cling to traditional religious values out of their love for God and/or Jesus, or their desire to be a pure and moral person, I find that deep down they are nearly all afraid. They are afraid of some final judgment, or a blow to their fragile human ego, or both. Judeo-Christianity in no shape or form teaches values and morals—the very words in the bible attest to that. In fact, those two words make not one appearance in the book. I also happen to find that the most pure and moral people are those who are non-religious persons, ones who do what is good and decent for the sake of doing what is good and decent, and not for the love/fear of a deity or two, or to stave off some phantom final judgment, or to reserve a nicer spot for all eternity for the same phantom afterlife.

Just as an alcoholic or a person addicted to gambling is in denial, so, too, are the religious people of the world in denial. They are in denial of the truth, and anything resembling the truth—anything that threatens their fear-driven, salvation-based, holier-than-thou views. Having faith in something does not make it true. Living in denial is easy; it is easy to explain and excuse any circumstance as the act of God rather than deal with the ramifications, repercussions, and reality of the situation, good or bad. It is harder for the frail human ego and psyche to accept that an uncountable amount of universal happenings must be taken at face value, and really are random. Faith does not make anyone stronger of character; rather it makes them weaker of reality. Faith does not make anyone better than another; rather it makes them think they are indeed better in many ways, especially morally.

To be cured of something one has to be sick with it. Religion is a sickness, a sort of mental illness, and henceforth a disease that preys upon only one of the creatures on planet Earth: mankind. Some diseases have no known cure, but religion is not one of those. Reason and truth work very well, but it depends upon the patient on how long it will take the cure to work.

So…. is religion a disease?

I believe it is. It is one that is transmitted after birth, and is not hereditary. Humans are born socially and—barring faulty wiring due to DNA, genomes, and pathologically related illness—mentally healthy. Human children are truly innocent, free of hatred and bigotry, and free of fear. Fear as in mortal fear—loud noises, separation anxiety, or that mean old dog next door may give them a spook, but they are free from true fear. They do not know hate, they are not influenced by a person's station or by the color of one's skin, nor do they acknowledge one's religious preference. Once children are able to comprehend complex thoughts and words, and when their parents and the people in direct contact with them on a daily basis infect them with religion, is when children lose their innocence.

To infect children with fear and lies does not produce healthy adults. To tell children that they must behave or believe in a certain way or else they will spend an eternity in a world of fire, pain, misery, and horrors with no possibility of escape is akin to child abuse. To lie to them about history, and tell them things that are not true let alone scientifically impossible, and have them believe that some unseen force can provide all they desire if only they believe a certain way is deluding them. A child must be reared with love, not fear. A child should be given encouragement, not fear-based, salvation-based agendas. Children should be raised to be self-sufficient, and not count on blessings, prayers, and divine intervention. The real world is cold and hard and brutal, and one must be strong enough to live in it, yet wise and compassionate enough to survive.

"I am now convinced that children should not be subjected to the frightfulness of the Christian religion.... If the concept of a father who plots to have His own son put to death is presented to children as beautiful and as worthy of society's admiration, what types of human behavior can be presented to them as reprehensible?"
Ruth Hurmence Green, 1915 - 1981

Like all diseases, religion needs a host in order to continue to exist. Once ingrained in the mind it attempts to corrupt it, control it, and ultimately use the host to infect others so that the infection may breed and multiply. The only known cure for this disease is truth and rationality. It is an uphill battle for the medicine to work, but once it does, the victim can be cured. How, you may ask, do I equate religion to an infectious disease? Humans are born without hate, as are all other forms of life. We learn hate as we live out our lives. We divide ourselves from people who are different as we grow, as our parents teach us, and as we learn from and imitate our peers. There are more ways to learn hate than just by religion alone, but nothing has the divisive power of religion.

The parents who are the most devout and the most adhering to their religion start the infection at an early age. As soon as the child can speak and form sentences the reagent of the disease enters their bloodstream, and by the time the child is old enough to reason for him or herself it is most likely too late. Well, I should not say that. It is never too late to throw off the shackles of mental and spiritual repression, but for the most part the disease of religion has taken hold by then. The grip by which said religion keeps its host bound is not love, not adoration, and definitely not reason; it is fear.

The parents who are less religious but still feel some sort of emotional or family-bound attachment to religion will raise their child/children with a little less of the disease-causing ingredient, but will infect them nonetheless. These parents, be they lax in their own beliefs—even downright unsure about them, but still clinging to them out of that same fear—or of mixed marriage in terms of religions and belief systems, will give the following and very lame argument for why they themselves are somewhat lax in their own faith—if they even have or follow a faith—but still choose to infect their child/children with religion. *"The child needs something, some sort of basis and moral code to build upon. When they get older they can figure it out for themselves, and choose what faith to follow."*

I know the sentiment very well; it is the same one my wife and I used to delude ourselves with while raising our child. My somewhat epiphany came when I realized that, no, the child does not need to be subjected to the lies and disease of what is not only untrue, but also by what is so divisive about religion. As a very, highly intelligent representative of the male species of *homo-sapiens* I did not mention this to my better half, and waited until this book was released to let my feelings be known. Not that my wife is religious by any means, but she whole-heartedly believes that statement above, and who am I to sleep on the couch?

"No, I don't know that atheists should be considered as citizens, nor should they be considered as patriots. This is one nation under God."
George W. Bush, 43rd President of the United States

This is from a commander in chief? Now hold on—I did vote for W, and I am not some unpatriotic, fanatic George Bush hater. I am a natural-born American. I pay taxes, I vote, and fully I support our troops. Do you see how divisive religion can be? Here we have our nation's leader telling me, an American citizen, that I am worthless. I should not even be considered a citizen of my own country because my religious beliefs differ from his. How many atheists and agnostics make up the brave members of our military, police, and fire fighters? Our own president is deeming those who are not Christian worthless human beings.

Aside from dividing us as a species, the disease of religion has one very serious side effect: delusions. The staggering amount of un-truths and nonsense preached by these two religions are just swallowed up as the pure and utter truths of life. Believing in things that are irrational and nonsensical is dangerous. Killing for them is even worse. Believing that there is an invisible human-like man in the sky watching and noting everything we say and do—and that it concerns itself with every trivial action—is an ego-inflating delusion. Believing that the laws of the universe can be stood upon their head because a supernatural force might make some rare and cryptic "miracle" happen is delusional. Believing that people can come back from the dead is delusional. Living a life in fear of some divine judgment or that a possible eternal fate of fire and torment is not healthy for the mind. Believing that prayer and faith can overcome a host of circumstances—most notably medical ones—is not healthy, let alone sane. It is not healthy for humans to be delusional and share society together. Not only for our sake, but our future's sake, and that of the children we bring into this world. How much have we been held back as a species due to the Judeo-Christian religion? What possible advances in science/technology, medicine, and the arts could we have procured?

Next to nothing is as divisive as is religion. Human kind's own xenophobia and feeble extent for true compassion and understanding comes a close second, but in dividing us as a species religion sits on the throne.

Shall we start with Christianity itself? How many branches are there on the tree that is Christianity? We have Christians, Catholics, Protestants, Episcopalians, Lutherans, Baptists, Southern Baptists, Mormons, Jews for Jesus, Seventh Day Adventists, Jehovah's Witnesses, The 12 Tribes, Pentecostals, Eastern-Orthodox, Russian Orthodox, Anglicans, Amish, Christian Scientists, Quakers, Shakers, non-denominational sects, born-again sects, evangelical sects, even Satanists (Satanism is a form of reverse Christianity), and more. This just proves that even among the devoted of the same religion that the people cannot get along. It is a version of "my dad can beat up your dad", only it is "my version of God and Christ is better than your version of God and Christ." Look at Ireland and how the bloody past between the Protestants and the Catholics has done wonders for the people there.

> *"When I told the people of Northern Ireland that I was an atheist, a woman in the audience stood up and said, "Yes, but is it the God of the Catholics or the God of the Protestants in whom you don't believe?"*
> Quentin Crisp, 1908 - 1999

Judaism has its own sects: orthodox, conservative, and reform. They pretty much get along aside from a few social, dietary, and dress code requirements, and each does share a common trait in that all study and worship the Torah. Each sect does not have its own book or own version of the Torah, and while they may differ on Talmudic interpretation, all three sects are basically one in the same. The same cannot be said for the various Christian sects, as many have their own books and bibles, each different in many ways from their counterparts.

Muslims, as a rule, hate Americans (and most all of the people of the world) not because we are Americans, but because we are not Muslims. We are infidels, and the Qu'ran calls for the murder and/or subjugation of all infidels—coincidentally, the bible says the same. Hitler hated many people, most notably the Jews. Some say Hitler was a Christian. Some say that Hitler was a bad Christian. The fact is that Hitler was multi-religious. He played the part of a dutiful Christian, saying he was doing the Lord's work in killing the killers of Christ, yet Hitler also invented a new religion for his 'ethnically superior' people. If you did not know already, please let me enlighten you on what the Nazi regime and religion was about.

Hitler preached that he and his people, the people of Germany and Germanic descent, were not just ordinary people, but descendents of the gods themselves. Not God, but the Nordic gods of legend. The blonde hair and light eyes were hallmarks of this race, and all others were to be subjugated under the 'new men' of the Nazi regime. As such Hitler enforced breeding programs and the Hitler Youth to ensure his progeny took over the world once he had conquered it. Ultimately, Hitler's regime took him away from his view of Christianity and replaced it with his new religion, with him as the savior. His own followers often compared Adolf Hitler to the figure of Jesus Christ. As I tangent here about Hitler, it boils down to another religion fueled by hate and intolerance. In the end I do not believe Hitler was a good or bad Christian, nor do I believe that he even bought into the rhetoric that he fed his people and by which he fueled his empire. I believe Hitler was an atheist or an agnostic at best. He used religion as the tool that it always is: a tool to rule, instill hatred, to divide, a tool to conquer, and a tool to quiet.

> *"Religion is regarded by the common people as true, by the wise as false, and by rulers as useful."*
> Seneca, circa 5 BCE – CE 65

So, where does the hate, fear, and separation actually end? More to the point, *when* will it end? As long as there are religions to divide us and set us apart we as a species will never know peace. As long as there are religions to hasten violence and intolerance while at the same time hindering our scientific advancement and personal growth people will always know hatred. As long as people buy into the lie of religion and its false promises we will never reach our true potential as a species. As long as people delude themselves and spread their delusions to their children we, as a functional society, will be repressed. Yes, there are forces at work other than religion that hold us back, make us hate, and repress mankind, but religion is at the forefront. Best of all, there is a cure for religion: truth. Faith cannot stand up to fact. Religion cannot stand up to science. If they both could, the world would still be in the dark ages.

It seems I have put my closing arguments in the very first chapter. I will have to work hard to come up with some better ones by the book's end. In order to comprehend what is in the next hundred pages or so, I ask that the reader be able to think rationally and critically. I often tend to remove myself from debates with religious people because I find that most religious people do not—cannot—think rationally. If they did they would not be religious, would they? Even if you are a very faithful person, please read my rants, my opinions, and what I bring to light in an open manner, read between the lines if you must, and let yourself see the message I am trying to convey.

"Each religion, so dear to those whose life it sanctifies, and fulfilling so necessary a function in the society that has adopted it, necessarily contradicts every other religion, and probably contradicts itself."
George Santayana, 1863 – 1952

Two: Discredit & Contradiction

Part I

To truly begin this book, before we get to anything else, we must discredit the bible. That in itself is not a very hard thing to do, for the bible is its own worst enemy. There is dishearteningly very little "good" in the Good Book. Too many people in this world rely on this work of man as the direct word of God, and treat it as in infallible source of wisdom, history, and human rights. The bible is a mixture of many things, but a manual for truth and accurate history, morals, and for human rights the bible is not. It is a sort of history book, chronicling some of the natural and man-made occurrences that have happened throughout recorded history. It is a rudimentary attempt at a science book, looking to explain why and how the world (and, ultimately, the universe) operated. Finally, its main purpose is a tool for control that the Romans used to secure their empire via the modus operandi of fear.

There is no real way to "win" a conversation, argument, or debate with a religious person, for they will not accept any facts. Faith is enough, and two plus two will always equal five to these people. There are always two questions I am asked by my religious friends and/or people I converse/debate with: If you do not follow the bible and do not believe in God, how can you have or make moral judgments? If there is no God, what purpose do you have? These two questions have very easy answers, and all one needs to do is calmly explain them.

When it comes to morals, I simply reply in such a fashion: If what you term as moral behavior comes from the bible, or the God spoken of therein, you are at a loss. If you obtain your morals from a book about a deity that requires animal and human sacrifice, demands the murdering of women and children, incites people to genocide, preaches hate, intolerance, and xenophobia, and rewards people only for what they think and believe but not what they do, then not only do I question your own set of morals, but I reject the very premise for your question.

Of purpose that, too, is an easy answer. I return the question back upon those who ask it. So, your only purpose is to kiss the rear end of a pair of cosmic beings and do good only to save yourself from punishment, and buy a better seat for a phantom afterlife? That is not purpose, but the reward for good behavior with a gun held to your temple. And here I thought my purpose was to do good by my fellow man despite their faith (or lack thereof), the color of their skin, the country of their birth, or their sexual preferences for the sole reason that this life is as precious as it is short, so do good in this life and worry about what or what does not happen after we die. By using the principles of their faith against the faithful of the God of Abraham, you cannot "lose" such a debate.

The main problem [I have] with the bible is that it is in no way a "good book". It is a work of fiction written by barbaric men with barbaric customs, irrationalized fears, unearthly longings, and no knowledge of the world on which they lived. The bible is a book of war, murder, intolerance, rules for slavery, rules for rape, rules for spoils of war, and an instigator of cannibalism, incest, polygamy, ritual human and animal sacrifice, and finally it tries to lay down

8

scientific laws that are unfounded, untrue, and barely rational. Worst of all is the deity who is the instigator of all the bible stands for, a tyrant king who claims to be loving, kind, benevolent, omnipotent and omniscient, but seems to know very little about anything and does not show any of the loving kindness or the benevolence it touts, rather it is an impatient, temperamental, and cruel deity.

The bible as we know it today is not the original work. To learn just how the bible came to be, one must be versed in its history, which too many believers are not. Prior to the early 300's AD, loose texts were in circulation accounting for the supposed life, times, and trial of Jesus Christ. Early converts to what was is now being called Christianity used these texts. Like Mithraism, another popular religion at that time in history, this new religion was trendy and was wining over people very, very quickly. The emperor of Rome's mother was an early convert, and she tried to convert her son as well, but failed. Emperor Constantine the Great only partially converted, and held many pagan beliefs until he died.

It was the 2nd century Turkish merchant, Marcion of Sinope—who was later branded a heretic for his dualistic views between Judaism and a budding Christianity—who offered that the writings should be united into an official church scripture. In 325 AD, Emperor Constantine I of Rome convened the First Council of Nicaea where a Bishop named Eusebius attended. It was decided, with the Bishop's input, that an official book of scripture was to be created, and uniformly used. Bishop Eusebius decided that only eighteen of the original texts should be used to constitute the bible. These books included the Old Testament, or Jewish Talmudic books, and in 331 AD Constantine commissioned the Bishop to craft the first Christian Bible. In 371 AD the official and now canonized Christian Bible was released and it included not eighteen, but some twenty-seven books in all, with many others being left out completely.

This canonized bible was in use for over one thousand years, and was not written in English. The texts were translated from Hebrew to Greek. Now we fast-forward 1300's England, where the historical figure of John Wycliffe comes into play. Mr. Wycliffe was an English theologian, and a translator. It is said that Mr. Wycliffe alone translated the entire New Testament into Queen's English. Wycliffe was a dissident from the Roman Catholic Church, and he is also noted as the father of Protestantism. In the year 1384 his translation of the New Testament was complete. The Torah, or Old Testament, was translated by Wycliffe's associates roughly at the same time. The life and times of John Wycliffe are very noted and detailed, and an entire book could be written about them alone. I highly suggest that anyone who is interested in history (and Christian History) read up on Mr. Wycliffe.

In the end, Wycliffe's stance against the papacy, and his own views and works with the bible, garnered for him many woes. He was a devilish opponent to debate, was a highly devoted to his work, and was stout in his own beliefs. He died in 1384 of sickness, but his story does not end there. In 1415 he was branded a heretic by the Church, his books and texts were burned, and his body was exhumed so that it could be burnt and its ashes spread across the River Swift.

Around the time of King James I of England, two-hundred years later, the Church of England still had no official and true canonized bible that was an accepted translation. In 1604 King James commissioned the Church to have a bible officially translated to his liking. Forty-seven scholars and translators toiled for seven years, and in 1611 the King James Bible was completed. With all the known Wycliffe versions collected and destroyed, this new bible was copied and distributed throughout the churches of England and their empire, and soon became the word of God for all English-speaking people, and soon the world.

"You do not need the Bible to justify love, but no better tool has been invented to justify hate."
Richard A. Weatherwax

In order to see the world for what it is, and to see how religion, as if it were some malevolent, nefarious and sentient beast, has played mankind like a deck of well-worn cards, we must discredit the only source of the Judeo-Christian argument, the bible. Once a person can see through the genocidal, nonsensical, un-scientific, and chauvinistic book can he/she begin to see these two religions in a new light. It is easier by far to just accept thinly-veiled and fear-motivated religions rather than to be brave and reject ancient ideas from an ancient people that have no place in a modern, cognitive-driven society. The big problem is that we have the ability, the freedom, and the scientific advances to be free and cognitive thinkers, but the hold that these two religions have over people is utterly astounding.

Why do so many people take the Old and New Testaments so solemnly, and believe they are both the "word of God"? It cannot be from a rational and critical standpoint. Despite any argument a religious person may put up in their defense, or in defense of God, the bible cannot stand up to reason and rationality. The book of Genesis alone shows how infantile man's own knowledge of the world was, as well as it shows what a load of nonsense the supposed "word of God" is. There are so many blunders, contradictions, and mistakes in Genesis that the only miracle that Judeo-Christianity can get credit for is this—anyone who fully reads the book of Genesis and stays a Jew or a Christian is a miracle.

The Old and New Testament are full of stories and ideas that we know are just not true. Most of what the bible says is pure fantasy and whim, written by men who knew nothing of science and the ways of the universe. One can read the bible, or any holy book for that matter, and see in it whatever they wish, extract whatever meaning or prophecy they care. Holy books are very versatile in that fashion, hence why they are all so ambiguous and non-succinct.

Aside from mistruths, the bible was mostly written by men to further their own agendas, which were control and money. The bible is also an astrological work as well as a religious one. Astrology was a big science of early man. Of the earth, man knew very little, always having explained anything that happened as acts of one god or another. The stars, however, were another story. The gods, thought ancient man, may have created them, but it was something man could track and chart. Man could identify with the stars, and like all the gods he ever created so did man anthropomorphize (adding human traits and characteristics to animals and inanimate objects) the stars.

The bible has become a catch-all for any argument on the behalf of any religious person. "Because it says so in the bible," and "the bible says" are in no way valid arguments, nor are they proof of anything but faith. Faith can never replace proof, nor can it prove the mystical. Many men and women better than I have cited obvious gaffes found within the pages of the bible. I hope I do not step on their toes or take credit for figuring out some of them. There are dozens of examples, and here are some rather simple ways to refute the bible and show it to be man-made nonsense:

- In Numbers 23:19 we learn that God never repents. In Exodus 32:14 God repents.

- In the book of Leviticus the bible tells us that bats are birds, rabbits chew cud like cows do, and that some birds and insects have four legs. This is all wrong, as we well know, yet this is a divinely-inspired work with **no** scientific errors?
- The book of 1 Kings tells us that Solomon had 40,000 stalls for his horses and his home had 2,000 baths. In 2 Chronicles Solomon had but 4,000 stables and 3,000 baths. Which is it?
- Exodus 33:20 says that there is no man that can live after seeing God's face. Genesis 32:30 tells a story of how a man saw God's face and his life was saved. Never mind the contradiction, the Ten Commandments says that man shall make no images of God and that God is not to be worshiped as such. If so then why would God have a face, and why would God Himself fashion one and "show" it to a man? What of the Cross, statues of the Virgin Mary, and the depictions of Jesus?
- Deuteronomy 24 specifically tells believers that people will not be guilty of the sins of their fathers. "Fathers shall not be put to death for their children, nor children put to death for their fathers; each is to die for his own sin". The first and biggest problem here is that Jesus supposedly died for all of mankind's sins, but does not Deuteronomy 24 rebuke that? Moreover, Leviticus 26:21 vividly describes how God will punish children and cattle for sins perpetrated by a single man/the father. "But if you will not listen to me and carry out all these commands, and if you reject my decrees and abhor my laws and fail to carry out all my commands and so violate my covenant, then I will do this to you: I will bring upon you sudden terror, wasting diseases and fever that will destroy your sight and drain away your life. You will plant seed in vain, because your enemies will eat it. I will set my face against you so that you will be defeated by your enemies; those who hate you will rule over you, and you will flee even when no one is pursuing you." If after all this you will not listen to me, I will punish you for your sins seven times over. I will break down your stubborn pride and make the sky above you like iron and the ground beneath you like bronze. Your strength will be spent in vain, because your soil will not yield its crops, nor will the trees of the land yield their fruit. "If you remain hostile toward me and refuse to listen to me, I will multiply your afflictions seven times over, as your sins deserve. I will send wild animals against you, and they will rob you of your children, destroy your cattle and make you so few in number that your roads will be deserted."

When one finishes reading Leviticus 26 all the way to the end at line 46 it is plain to see that the God of Judeo-Christianity is but a vain, fear-mongering, whiny, petulant, childish, jealous, bloodthirsty bully. A perfect being would have none of these traits, let alone scare the life out of its subjects with them.

Also notice how in the verse above God says He will set His "face" against you. If no man can live after seeing His face, what need has God for all the other threats? Won't just showing His face across the lands kill everything?

"The god of the Bible measures up to the level of a petty and vicious tyrant. The god of the bible punishes babies for the sins of their parents (Exodus 20:5, 34:7; Numbers 14:18; 2 Samuel 12:13-19); punishes people by causing them to become cannibals and eat their children (2 Kings 6:24-33, Lamentations 4:10-11); gives people bad laws, even requiring the sacrifice of their firstborn babies, so that they can be filled with horror and know that god is their lord (Ezekiel 20:25-26); causes people to believe lies so that he can send them to hell (2 Thessalonians 2:11), and many other atrocities, far too many to list here. It would not be hard to measure up to, and exceed, that level of moral purity. Atheists surpass it every day."
Doug Krueger

As I had stated above, Genesis is a treasure trove of mistakes. To refute God's supposed omniscience all one need to do is read through Genesis, the first book of the bible. If God is omniscient, the whole book of Genesis becomes irrelevant and the religion is shown as a charade. How so?

- You have a supposedly omniscient God who creates a world and a few humans. The humans are made from dust and dirt.
- He places trees and animals upon this world, but for some reason commands the humans not to eat from once specific tree. The animals and humans get along swimmingly. Meanwhile, God Himself cannot tell bats from birds, and has no clue exactly which animals have feet and wings and in what combination. He also despises many of his new creations and deems them to be "abominations".
- A talking snake convinces a human woman to eat from the forbidden tree. When she does, God is surprised and becomes irate.
- God curses the snake, curses all the humans—especially the females of the species—and changes the world, making animal and man foes. This is where it gets funny. God cursed all snakes to henceforth crawl on their bellies. How did they move prior to this? Did they fly? Hop on their tails?
- A while later two of the humans, siblings, come to odds, and one kills the other. God then asks the killer where his sibling is (why does God not know?) In Genesis Eve is the only woman. How do all her sons procreate if not by incest? The original books of the bible do not tell.
- Humans lived for hundreds and hundreds of years, which we know is not possible. In fact we know that humans of this era generally lived to be forty-five to sixty-five years in age, and were shorter than we are now. It is only in modern times that humans live eighty-five years of age or older, and that we are as tall as we have ever been. Just look at old suits of armor and medieval castle doorways for the proof.
- Moving on, God is not satisfied with His work, so He sends a flood to kill everyone and all the animals save for a few of each species—99% of which are not native to the desert. Why bother with a flood? Seems like a waste of energy—just showing His face across the land would have been quicker, easier, and more economical in terms of energy.
- One question I have is what did God plan to do about marine life? A flood would not kill a single fish, mollusk, crustacean, or sea-going mammal like dolphins, whales, and possibly seals, nor would it kill many (if any at all) crocodiles, caiman, and alligators, and even most snakes. If you follow this logic, it stands to

argue that God deemed all sea-going animals to be fine (regardless of if they had scales or not) and worthy of surviving His flood. Then again, many of these animals are considered abominations by God, so why did they survive the flood?

I could go on about the blunder of Genesis, but there is no need. The story of Genesis demonstrates without a shadow of a doubt that the bible is work of fiction, and beyond that the god it portrays is not omniscient in the least. God seems to know not the future, not what these humans will do, and tries to erase His mistakes with a flood. What happened to a perfect creator? Genesis belies error, fallacy, and mistake after mistake, not perfection.

The bible has all the attributes of a book written by a species that knew nothing of science and of the world on which it lived, yet tried to explain it. It has all the attributes of a book written by the male desire to be dominant over females and animals. It is a justification for greed, blood lust, and sexual desires not only allowed and excused, but demanded by the deity.

It is not very difficult to discount the bible, for if you read through it the book contradicts itself a staggering amount of times. Never mind all the killing and genocide, setting aside the commands by God for animal and human sacrifice, allowing for all the hate and intolerance, if you can look at all that and still call the bible the "good book", what of all the following, blatant contradictions?

Acts 1:24 "Then they prayed, "Lord, you know everyone's heart. Show us which of these two you have chosen."
Psalm 139 "You perceive my thoughts from afar. You discern my going out and my lying down; you are familiar with all my ways. Before a word is on my tongue you know it completely, O LORD"
Jeremiah 32:27 ""I am the LORD, the God of all mankind. Is anything too hard for me?"
Here are just three examples of God's power. He knows what is in everyone's heart, He knows what everyone does and will do before they do it or says it, and nothing is too hard for Him, because He is God. It makes sense if God is a transcendent and omniscient being. If so, please explain the passages below.

Deuteronomy 13:3 "You must not listen to the words of that prophet or dreamer. The LORD your God is testing you to find out whether you love him with all your heart and with all your soul."

Deuteronomy 8:3 "Remember how the LORD your God led you all the way in the desert these forty years, to humble you and to test you in order to know what was in your heart, whether or not you would keep his commands."

Genesis 22:12 "Do not lay a hand on the boy," he said. "Do not do anything to him. Now I know that you fear God, because you have not withheld from me your son, your only son."

Job 11 "For He knows false men, And He sees iniquity without investigating"

Judges 1:19 "The LORD was with the men of Judah. They took possession of the hill country, but they were unable to drive the people from the plains, because they had iron chariots. As Moses had promised, Hebron was given to Caleb, who drove from it the three sons of Anak. The Benjamites, however, failed to dislodge the Jebusites, who were living in Jerusalem; to this day the Jebusites live there with the Benjamites."

God is omniscient and omnipotent. He knows the hearts of humans, knows what they will do, say, or think before they do it, and is all-powerful; "Is anything too hard for me?" are God's own words. Yet He needs to test people to see if they love Him, or will obey Him. That is not

omniscience. That is just the opposite, and is, moreover, insecurity. He is with the men of Judah as they go into battle, yet Judah's forces were defeated. If nothing is too hard for Him and there is nothing He cannot do, then why were Judah's forces defeated? God can create or do anything, but cannot help a few mortals take a hill? That is not omnipotence. That is incompetence.
To further cite some contradictions pertaining to God's power and omnipotence, we can take from the following verse.

Isaiah 40:28 "Do you not know? Have you not heard? The LORD is the everlasting God, the Creator of the ends of the earth. He will not grow tired or weary."
Directly contradicting that is this. Exodus 31:17 "It will be a sign between me and the Israelites forever, for in six days the LORD made the heavens and the earth, and on the seventh day he abstained from work and rested." Another verse is found in Genesis "It will be a sign between me and the Israelites forever, for in six days the LORD made the heavens and the earth, and on the seventh day he abstained from work and rested."

Perhaps it is just me, but did God not say He is God, the omnipotent God for Whom nothing is too hard? As such, why would He rest? There are so many contradictions found in the bible that an entire book could be written about them alone. Here are a few more examples in a more curt way to show that the good book is its own worst enemy.

- Matthew 7:8 and Proverbs 8:17 tell us that all who seek God shall find him, all who knock will have the door opened, and all who ask of Him shall be answered. Proverbs 1:28, however, says that though some may seek Him diligently they will not find Him. I guess God fibbed.
- In James 1 we learn God does not tempt men or deceive, for this is not what He does. "God cannot be tempted with evil, neither tempteth he any man". In Genesis, Jeremiah 20:7 and Matthew 6:13 God has tempted, tested, or deceived men and/or has the same men, who know God does not do these things, begging for them not to happen. "And it came to pass after these things, that God did tempt Abraham," Genesis: 22. Moreover, if God does not tempt humans, what is the deal with the apple tree in Eden? Why put it there and then order Adam and Even not to eat from it? A snake tempted Eve, but was not the snake a creation of God, and ultimately acting upon God's will?
- Mark 8:35 quotes Jesus as saying "Whosoever shall lose his life for my sake and the gospels the same shall save it". There were no gospels during the life of Jesus, and the gospels only appeared after Jesus' death and supposed resurrection. That makes all the gospels hearsay, and ultimately fallible information at best.
- In Genesis 1:16 it tells how the stars were created after the earth itself was. In Job 38:4 we learn that the stars were made before the earth. In Genesis 5:3 we learn that Enoch was six generations apart from Adam, but in Jude 14 it tells that Enoch was seven generations from Adam. In Genesis 5:24 the story tells us about how Enoch did not die, but instead was taken by God to heaven. In John 3 the bible tells us that no man ascends into heaven. In genesis 11 Abraham is 135 years old when he leaves Haran, but in Genesis 12 Abraham was 75 years old when he left Haran. It seems nothing in Genesis—let alone the rest of the bible—can be counted on as neither valid nor solid, and this is the inspired words of a perfect God?

14

- Deuteronomy 21 and 24 says that a man may divorce his wife if he "No longer delighteth…" in her. Jesus then says, in Matthew 5:32 that the only way people can divorce is through acts of adultery. Then, reverting to the Talmud, it says that adultery is grounds for the killing of men and women.
- Jesus was supposed to be a teacher of peace. He is famous for His "turn the other cheek" philosophy. These lines can be found in Matthew 5:39, Matthew 6:38, and Matthew 26:52. Now look at Luke 22 where Jesus tells people to take up arms for a fight, and then in John 2;15 where Jesus uses a whip to drive people out of a temple. The final nail in the coffin for Jesus as a peaceful man-god comes in Matthew 10:34. "I came not to send peace but a sword" are the words of Jesus.
- The most telling line I can think of to besmirch the entire Christian religion can also bring it to its knees should it try and refute it. The verse comes from Psalm 103. "The LORD is compassionate and gracious, Slow to anger and abounding in loving kindness. He will not always strive with us, Nor will He keep His anger forever." Then Psalm 30 adds "For His anger is but for a moment, His favor is for a lifetime". Is this the same God who sends souls to Hell on a whim, to be tortured and tormented for all of eternity? This same Hell that from which there is no escape, no reprieve? Is this the same God that is slow to anger yet a fig tree barren of fruit sends him into a rage? The same God that created all of mankind but ones that pray to other gods should be slaughtered? Is this the kind God who, after creating the world, tried to drown all its occupants? To belabor the human qualities in God, a god—more importantly God—should be beyond any petty, human emotions, especially hate and intolerance. If not it is not a deity worth devoting oneself to.

Psalms 30 and 103 really say it all. If you have a decent argument to defend the two Psalms versus the idea of Hell and eternal punishment (and such punishment for simply thinking and believing differently), then please give it. A defense of "God works in mysterious ways" and "who are we to question God?" hold no water, and are illegitimate and childish attempts at a defense.

In any case, there are dozens more examples of how the bible contradicts itself with glaringly obvious mistakes, oversights, and flat out blunders. It shows that the Holy Scripture is a work of man, not divinely inspired, and an imperfect item.

Part II

The bible is to be the word of God, a divinely inspired text. In whatever fashion the words went from God's cosmic lips to man's unsteady hand, the book is supposed to be the be all and end all of scientific and spiritual knowledge. If divinely inspired by the perfect creator why is the bible full of glaringly, painfully obvious wrongs? Why would God not only inspire men to write down what is untrue, but also allow them to do so and never correct it? Is it not one of the Ten Commandments "thou shall not bear false witness?"

We know the earth is not 6,000 or 10,000 years old like the bible says it is.

We know man did not come from a pile of dirt and dust and that woman was not made from the rib of a man.

We know humans cannot live to be centuries more in age.

We know animals, like snakes and donkeys, cannot talk.

We know a flood did not destroy most of world and all of its inhabitants.

We know animals like the polar bear, Kodiak bear, opossum, platypus, gypsy moth, mountain lion, penguin, koatamundi, kangaroo, panda, blue jay, American alligator, puffin, gray wolf, musk ox, Atlantic salmon, American bison, dodo bird, arctic fox, northern hellgrammite, wolverine, koala, diamondback, jaguar, orangutan, and thousands of others were not found in or around the deserts or even in the Mediterranean or in Africa, and that could not have been collected and put on any large boat.

We know dinosaurs and hundreds of thousands of different creatures existed long before mankind ever did. We also know they did not exist alongside man and modern mammals, nor did they board the fictional Noah's ark.

We know the earth revolves around the sun.

We know a man cannot survive in the belly of a "fish" for 3 days, and that whales and sea-going mammals are indeed not fish.

We know the universe was not made in 6 days.

We know bats are not members of the bird family.

We know no birds exist that have four feet.

We know all insects have six legs, and not four.

We know no other non-avian and non-insect animals have four feet *and* wings.

We know snakes do not nor ever did eat "dust".

We know there are new things under the sun (to paraphrase from the bible), and that we do *not* know all that there is to know.

"One of the most frightening things in the Western world, and in this country in particular, is the number of people who believe in things that are scientifically false. If someone tells me that the earth is less than 10,000 years old, in my opinion he should see a psychiatrist."
Francis Crick, 1916 - 2004

Ancient man in his limited, flat-Earth wisdom could not have known about the world outside of the Asiatic and African deserts. Anything beyond Rome or Asia was just too much for the minds at the time; that much is evident. Likewise, the same minds that penned the Old Testament could not envision the future, and know that one day men would begin to learn the truth about the planet, the stars, and of the universe. Science was as strange to them as a bowl of salad is to a lioness. Magic, myth, and religion explained all there was to know.

How do people reconcile such things yet keep their faith? How can someone who believes in God and what the bible preaches also believe in dinosaurs? It is belittling of human intelligence to state that the bones of dinosaurs were put there by God to test our faith. God is supposed to be omniscient and, as we learned in the bible, knows what is in our hearts and minds. Why, then, would He put the bones there to test and tempt us? (Especially when God is not a tempter of man, as He claims). It is a circular paradox, and shows that God does not exist. How does a rational, thinking person go about reconciling anything that is an obvious mistruth, or proven to be incorrect, and still keep their faith? What excuses must such a person make on the behalf of God? Why do they make excuses would be a better question. If you need to make an excuse to reconcile faith with modern-day facts, facts win and the religion you excuse shows

16

its fraud. God should not need any excuses to be made on His behalf, yet as soon as one is made the concept of God becomes irrelevant.

In any case, the bible cannot stand on its laurels. It is not a viable source of information. It cannot stand up to any measure of science or examination as so many apologists and defenders say it can. The bible is obviously not divinely-inspired and can only be called such if its divine inspiration comes from a deity who is neither omniscient or omnipotent, and lacks even the most basic knowledge of the universe in which it exists.

"Faith means not wanting to know what is true."
Nietzsche, 1844 – 1900

Part III: Of Prophecies

Defenders of the Judaeo-Christian faith, especially the Christians, tout the bible as a prophetic marvel, and say that the bible has predicted thousands of occurrences that have since happened. Defenders marvel at these so-called prophecies, but the bible is a loose book; you can read at and make it say almost anything you wish. In fact, the men who wrote the gospels very conveniently hand-picked the parts of the Talmud they wanted to create into self-fulfilling (or already fulfilled, once they were through) prophecies. A rational, critical mind knows prophecies are as real as unicorns. The bible contradicts itself more than anything, and even its prophecies are not reliable. The easiest one to dismantle is the prophecy of Isaiah 7. God tells of how a virgin will give birth to a son. "Therefore the Lord himself will give you a sign: The virgin will be with child and will give birth to a son, and will call him Immanuel"

I have never heard of the figure known as Immanuel Christ. Have you? I have never ever heard of anyone famous or infamous named Immanuel that was born of a virgin. You would think that would garner some attention. I have, however, heard of a Jesus Christ. Perhaps this Jesus is the one prophesized in Matthew 1? The long version is such: "This is how the birth of Jesus Christ came about: His mother Mary was pledged to be married to Joseph, but before they came together, she was found to be with child through the Holy Spirit. Because Joseph her husband was a righteous man and did not want to expose her to public disgrace, he had in mind to divorce her quietly. But after he had considered this, an angel of the Lord appeared to him in a dream and said, "Joseph son of David, do not be afraid to take Mary home as your wife, because what is conceived in her is from the Holy Spirit. She will give birth to a son, and you are to give him the name Jesus, because he will save his people from their sins." All this took place to fulfill what the Lord had said through the prophet: "The virgin will be with child and will give birth to a son, and they will call him Immanuel"which means, "God with us." When Joseph woke up, he did what the angel of the Lord had commanded him and took Mary home as his wife. But he had no union with her until she gave birth to a son. And he gave him the name Jesus."

Is this a mistake and/or contradiction all within the same verse, or is it me? Does God not tell people He will send a son who will be named Immanuel? If so, why would He deem to name the son Immanuel in one stanza, Jesus in the next, and then a few lines later the son is again called Immanuel when the name is Jesus? Did God not proofread His own self-inspired work? Was this verse in Matthew a cover-up to make the figure of Jesus acceptable to the masses when He was already prophesized to be named Immanuel?

17

Another fallacy is found in the book of Matthew 27:9. Here we have this prophecy: "Then what was spoken by Jeremiah the prophet was fulfilled: "They took the thirty silver coins, the price set on him by the people of Israel, and they used them to buy the potter's field, as the Lord commanded me." If anyone can show where in the book of Jeremiah this prophecy is or is fulfilled, well…call me pisher (it's an old Yiddish saying. Look it up).

To widen the rift of non-fulfilled prophecies we can look at Romans 1:3 and Acts 2:30. In those books we learn that the messiah must be a physical descendant of King David. If you read through the books of Matthew and Luke you will see that Jesus descended from David through Joseph, and Joseph was not even his natural father since Jesus was conceived via the Immaculate Conception and His father was God. This prophecy has no way of being fulfilled.
Isaiah 7:16 prophesized that before Jesus would mature both Jewish countries would be decimated. This is never fulfilled with the coming and going of Jesus anywhere in the New Testament or in history.

There are, of course, more unfulfilled prophecies, but we must go on without them. The fact is that a person can read any religious text, or the back of a Nestle Toll House Cookie bag, and glean whatever they want to out of it.

People should also note that so much was lost in the original translation from Hebrew to Greek, and then from Greek to English. As Thomas Paine pointed out more than two hundred years ago, the words prophet and prophecy were mistranslations and misunderstood terms. The original intent and meaning of the words to the people of the day around the time Jesus supposedly lived were different. Prophet meant poet, and prophecy meant poetry. To prophesize meant to make poems and music. What bearing does that have? It means the bible is not full of prophets but rather poets and musicians, bards and entertainers, not seers and mystics (which, by the way, the bible says to kill).

"Organized religion is a sham and a crutch for weak-minded people who need strength in numbers. It tells people to go out and stick their noses in other people's business."
Jesse "The Body" Ventura, 1951 –

Part IV: Banned but Not Forgotten

More than ten books were banned from the final edition of the bible as it was translated to Greek. For hundreds of years after the supposed death of Jesus, numerous texts of the life, trials, and death of Jesus Christ existed in and about the lands ruled by Rome. Many of these books and texts were banned well before King James' scholars went to work. Just what books were banned and edited out of the final Christian Bible? Here is a rundown of some of them.

The Book of Adam and Eve: Basically a re-run of Genesis, which has Satan running amok in the Garden of Eden, tempting Eve numerous times as the snake, and enraging God by not bowing down to Adam when told to do so, and then erecting a huge altar in Heaven for his own glory. For such actions He is cast out, and banished to Hell.
The Book of Enoch: A descendant of Noah, this book describes the life and times of Enoch and how Enoch is presented with much astrological knowledge. This book also expands the books of Deuteronomy and Genesis and details how God's angels lusted after human women, and taught mortal man to forge weapons. It was left out because the Book of Enoch was deemed too odd.

The Gospel of Nicodemus: This book, supposedly written in the 4th century AD, relates to Jesus, His trial, His execution, and His time spent in Hell. It was left out because church officials deemed it a forgery to gain converts.

The Gospel of Mary: This book professes Mary Magdalene to be a credited apostle and receives unique teachings from Jesus Christ. The book and its teachings were deemed not orthodox enough and it was subsequently omitted from the bible.

The Proto-Gospel of James: This book reveals many contradictions to the original New Testament, especially in relation to Mary's virginal status. It was omitted because the church officials felt it was detracting and chronologically incorrect.

The Book of Jubilees: Written to explain away some of the obvious blunders in Genesis (notably how Adam and Even were said to have three sons and no daughters, so how did Cain take and impregnate a wife, and where did all the other humans come from if not Eve having incestuous relations with her sons). This book was deemed unworthy and too illicit.

The Proto-Gospel of Thomas: Written of Jesus' youth, this book details how Jesus was likely a "brat" as a child, and was omitted.

The Scriptures of Nag Hammadi: These scriptures were found in a jar in the hills of Nag Hammadi, Egypt, in 1945. The documents contained more than fifty texts written by supposedly heretical Christians. They believed that the world and all things physical were the creation of a god that was not God, but an evil and lesser god. They wrote that true salvation comes from transcending this world and awakening the inner god within all of us. Also found with these texts was the Gospel of Mary.

The 1st and 2nd Apocalypse of Peter: These two books mirrored the Revelation of John. They also give a vivid description of what it is like in Hell and the text even suggests a way for sinners to win reprieve from Hell. That, of course, would not do, and so the 1st book was banned. The second book deals with the death of Jesus, and casts him in a way that church officials deemed was unfit, and the book was labeled as heretical.

More than just these texts were either banned and/or omitted, and that is just the start. I could go on about how the bible was written, re-written, translated numerous times, and I belabor this to show how the bible is man's work, not God's. Man crafted and tailored the bible, and he edited and reworked it to suite his own needs and tastes. If the holy scriptures are the words of God, how dare mortal man edit them, pick and choose what to print and what not to print? Is that not heresy?

"Whenever we read the obscene stories, the voluptuous debaucheries, the cruel and tortuous executions, the unrelenting vindictiveness with which more than half the Bible is filled, it would be more consistent that we call it the word of a demon than the word of God. It is a history of wickedness that has served to corrupt and brutalize mankind; and, for my part, I sincerely detest it, as I detest everything that is cruel."
Thomas Paine, 1737 – 1809

Three: A Little Trip Down Memory Lane - History 101

Before we get deeper into Judeo-Christianity, we must look back to where it all came from. The world's first known and recorded monotheism was Zoroastrianism, also known as Mazdaism. No, primitive societies did not worship Japanese cars and the words "zoom, zoom" were never uttered in reverent prayer. Zoroastrianism was the teachings of the prophet Zarathustra who dwelled in Iran during the tenth century BC. His teachings spread as far as India, but it was never a dominating religion in terms of the numbers of its followers. In fact, Zoroastrianism is still practiced to this day and it is among the oldest surviving religions. The Jewish and the Christian religions have many things in common with Zoroastrianism, and Zoroastrianism has had more influence on other monotheistic religions than any other of its kind. Zoroastrianism revered the god Ahura Mazda, the transcendent creator who was never created Himself. Idolized as fire and the sun, Ahura Mazda represents truth, order, kindness, and free will. From Iran we travel to Egypt and go back to the Eighteenth Dynasty of the New Kingdom, or about 1,350 BC. Here we meet Pharaoh Amenhotep IV, also known as Akhenaten. His fame, or his infamy, rather, is why most people have never heard of this unique Pharaoh.

Amenhotep IV's name and works were stricken from most of Egypt's long history. Why? Amenhotep IV was the first and only Pharaoh to not only practice monotheism, but enforced it upon the dynasty during his reign. It was known as the Amarna period. Amenhotep IV believed that there was but one god, the god Aten, God of the Sun, God of Creation and Light. Temples were erected to this one mighty god, and stripped of power and station were the many priests and priestesses of the other now abandoned gods. Some historians say this move was purely political, that Amenhotep IV used this power play to not only shift power from the clergy to himself, but it was a monetary play as well. Amenhotep IV used this additional income to strengthen his military and secure his reign.

The monotheistic rule of Amenhotep IV did not last long. He died an untimely death in the year 1,361 BC and his rule was cut short. He was surpassed on the throne by Ramesses the Great. Ramesses's first order of business, and his most notable achievement, was that he utterly brought the Amarna period of Egypt's history to an end. All temples of Aten were demolished. Tablets and papyrus pertaining to the era were destroyed. Power was put back into the hands of the priesthood. Most statues and carvings of Amenhotep IV were turned into rubble. Writings on temple walls were destroyed and re-worked. The great pantheon of Egypt's gods was restored, and Ramesses vied to bring back the glory of the days before Amenhotep IV. Why Ramesses did this is a topic of debate. Was he truly afraid of his gods of old, that the great pantheon would take revenge on his people? The Armana period of Egypt's was ripe with plague, famine, and sickness. Were the forgotten gods responsible? Was it a socio-economic move to destroy monotheism? Was it a bargain he struck with the priesthood? Either way Ramesses must have had a darned good reason to erase monotheism from his nation and revert to polytheism.

What is important to note is that during the days of Amenhotep IV and this time of monotheism is that many of the traits we see in modern, as well as historic, Judeo-Christianity came from the time of this Pharaoh's rule and religious ways. An example is the idea of the trinity; the basis for a holy trinity is not unique to Christianity. In fact, as we will get into later, there is not much at all that Christianity can claim as unique. In this case, Amenhotep IV called Aten the God Supreme. Aten, also called Amun, however, was given three different personas. His trinity was himself as Aten/Amun, the transcendental who was there before creation and was above all and so he was hidden from view. Re or Ra was Aten's face, as in the disk of the sun. Ptah was his body or "primordial mound," the earth.

I have mentioned Amenhotep IV's version of this trinity for two reasons. One is that it ultimately predates the Christian religion. Another reason is that of the Hebrews and of Judaism. Judaism, like Egyptian mythology, predates Christianity. Moreover Judaism is the wellspring of Christianity, but it is apparent that Judaism is solely monotheistic; there is no trinity whatsoever. The Romans mixed bits and pieces from many religions when they solidified Christianity by writing the bible.

Like the Egyptians, the Romans had a great pantheon of gods and goddesses. The Roman religion itself was formed by assimilating older religions into its own, taking so very much from various cultures, a main one being the Etruscans.

The Etruscan people passed from Babylon to Greece and then to Rome in the early days of Rome's history. Their culture was absorbed along the way, but nowhere more so than in Rome. The Etruscan religion dealt with a triumvirate of powerful gods. Tinia, Uni, and Menerva. Tinia was the Etruscan equivalent of Jupiter and Zeus; god of the sky and of lightning. Uni the Mother-Goddess was akin to Hera and Juno or Greece and Rome, and Uni was the wife of Tinia. Menerva, the third of the trinity, was Goddess of Wisdom, War, and Commerce, paralleled with Athena. When the Etruscan people became completely assimilated into Roman Empire their religions were intertwined, and the idea of the trinity became typical in Rome and with Roman religion. Even though the Etruscan trinity, and ultimately the Roman, dealt with separate gods and goddesses, it shows how religious traditions were not only passed on, but adopted by the people living in the BC era.

"Christianity did not destroy paganism, it adopted it."
Will Durant, 1885 – 1981

Since we know that the idea of the trinity did not come from the Hebrews where did it come from if not the religions of the time? If not from Amenhotep IV and his monotheistic trinity, and if not from the Etruscan and/or Roman and Greek trinities, then from where? Should we go back further in time to the Sumerian and Assyrian pantheons of gods, both of which predate even the Hebrew religion and had triumvirates of their most powerful gods? We also know that the trinity of Christendom did not originate in the bible. Jesus never speaks of it in any of the books, and nowhere in the New Testament is the trinity mentioned or referred to. In fact, the word trinity did not come into being until more than a century after the figure of Jesus Christ's supposed death and resurrection.

Quintus Septimius Florens Tertullianus, although history knows him best as just Tertullian, he was one of the first Christian apologists, and he invented the word 'trinity', its meaning in relation to the Christian religion and further had it added to the Latin language. Seeing as how Tertullian lived from 160 to 225 AD it is not possible that the term was present prior to that and certainly not in the Old or New Testaments. Going back to the Hebrews and to the Egyptians living during the time of Pharaoh Amenhotep IV in the Amarna era, we have another interesting possibility. Do I believe that the Torah, like the New Testament, is the absolute truth? Of course not. Both are works of men; scared, mortal men who knew as much about science as a chipmunk knows about plumbing. I do believe, however, that where there is smoke there is fire, and that the stories and parables of both Old and New Testament must have some small, relevant story to base some of their mistruths upon. Exodus is a prime example in this case. While we can get into the debate of the Exodus later in the book, it is here that we can see—or at least I can see—from where the Jewish faith had its roots.

When Amenhotep IV died, and Ramesses took the throne, we know he immediately began to dismantle all of Amenhotep's work. Living in Egypt at that time were many people who were not Egyptian born. There were Hittites, Assyrians, Babylonians, Phoenicians, Greeks, and especially the Hyksos (a nomadic people of the Nile delta who many believe are the true Jews of lore). Some of this huge melting pot of people were slaves and some free citizens of the Egyptian empire. Undoubtedly, many among them were followers of the Cult of Aten.

It is more than plausible that, when Amenhotep IV's reign came to an end, they would have found themselves in a precarious situation. If they were true believers they would be left with three choices; go underground and pray not to be found out, assimilate back into the polytheism of Egypt, or leave the city altogether and make a new home elsewhere. From what history tell us—and not the history of the Torah or the bible—it seems that option three seemed the most viable, and so an exodus of sorts may indeed have taken place. We can never be sure of the exact number of people who fled the fall of the Armana era, or how many years it took them to relocate and rebuild their society, but it is certainly possible that it happened. Throughout history, people have always left religiously oppressive areas to seek greener pastures. The Pilgrims did it when they departed England for the New World, so is it a stretch to say that earlier peoples did so?

If hundreds or thousands of people left Armana era Egypt to seek a better life, there would have been a mass of people living pretty much a lawless, mixed-religious life. Since in no way, shape, or form do I buy into the story of how the figure of Moses parted a sea and led tens of thousands of people to a new home (which took forty years to find) we have to assume that people did what people do when no kings, queens, and politicians with military back-up is there to enforce the laws; they went primal. Again, to control and quiet the people the smartest and the most authoritative of this mass of people brought out the big guns when it comes to crowd control—religion.

You have a mass of people. Let us assume the majority are Aten worshipers. It is also possible that some of the people were polytheists from the time before the Armana era. We can also assume that there were Assyrian and Babylonian people here. Mix all these beliefs together, reinvent here, twist and tweak and reshape there, and from the ashes of Aten worship comes Judaism. It has all the basic signs of Assyrian and Egyptian monotheistic values (slavery, war, rape, a blood-thirsty deity, male domination and female subservience) with some new ones added in to calm and quiet the common people, as Napoleon put it.

The point of this historical diatribe is to add all the ingredients to the mix. We have our Assyrian, Phoenician, Sumerian, and Egyptian base for monotheism, our Hebrews/Hyskos and our Etruscans for seasonings, and our oven that is the heated environment of expanding and ever-changing politically-driven empires. The meal itself is served to the Romans, hungry for power and hungry to quiet the masses of common people it is taxing and enslaving to death. Coming into contact with all of these people and their different religions is the Roman Empire.

Now that we have established that Rome had not only come into contact with mixed theisms of the Assyrian lands, and that Roman mythology itself had actually been an assimilation of several cultures and religions, it is easy to see where the Christianity's roots came from. Roman Emperor Constantine and his royal cabinet—most all of them converts, and some probably still un-admitted polytheists—are responsible for the New Testament portion of the bible and not the Hebrews, not the Greeks, nor any other people. The New Testament was written many decades after the figure of Jesus Christ supposedly lived and died, making everything not only hearsay, but making the timeline of the religion grounds for its own dismantling. Nothing is "revelation" about the bible, as it is all second, third, and forth-hand accounts. It is even quite debatable if even the apostles wrote their own texts as each expresses different accounts of the life of Jesus, and not one the books of Mark, Luke, Matthew, and John gels with one another. Again, all this is for a later chapter.

The roots of monotheism are old, but not original to the Jews or to the Christians. The two, however—and like all other claims of all other religions—would have you believe that theirs is the true path, the only path, and the correct path.

"All children are atheists—they have no idea of God."
Paul-Henri, Baron d'Holbach, 1723 – 1789

Four: Knock, knock.....anybody home?

A man is climbing a mountain alone. He nears the summit and it is only a few feet from his goal. He smiles, knowing all his hard work and training will pay and that he will have conquered the stoic, unforgiving pile of rock. As he reaches for the ledge he loses his grip and he begins to slide down. His Harness snaps and breaks, his lines are all cut and fall away. In desperation he reaches out and grabs hold of a tangle of roots that is jutting out from the side of the mountain. The man takes several breaths to steady his nerves and his mind kicks into gear. Roots mean trees. Trees atop a mountain means life, and possibly people. He calls out.

"Hello! I need help. Please! Is there anybody up there?"

He waits for a reply, but hears nothing. He repeats his plea and suddenly hears a voice coming from seemingly everywhere.

"I am here," the voice calmly says.

"Oh, thank God. I cannot hold on much longer. Please, throw me a line. Help me."

The voice answers. "I am the Lord, God, and I will help you."

The man almost weeps with joy. He awaits the roots to take hold of him and lift him up. Perhaps a strong wind will carry him to safety. Perhaps, even, the hand of God will rescue him and place him atop the mountain.

"Let go of the roots," the voice says, "and I will save you."

"What? Let go?" the man asks. "I will fall to my death."

"Do you have faith, my son?"

"Of course I do."

"Then let go. I will save you."

The man thinks for a quick second, and then replies, "Is there anybody else up there?"

*****

My father used to tell that joke all the time. He is a religious man, raised in an orthodox Jewish home in Brooklyn, New York. Suffice to say that, despite his upbringing and convictions, he became reformed by his mid twenties. He is still a deeply religious man, but has always kept his beliefs and his convictions to himself. I do not ever recall him preaching to me, my sisters, or to anyone. His affair with his god was and is a private one. But he loves that joke.

So, is there a god? Is there an omniscient, omnipotent, omnipresent, transcendent being out there? That is the twenty-five thousand dollar question, the one that people have been debating since man first developed language and thought. Book after book has been written in defense and defiance of this subject. You are reading yet another right now, and a thousand more are sure to come after this meager attempt at the age-old argument.

"If God did not exist, it would be necessary to invent him."
Voltaire, 1694 – 1778

24

"I reverse the phrase of Voltaire, and say that if God really existed, it would be necessary to abolish him."
Mikhail Bakunin, 1814 – 1776

To believe in God, the god of the Jews and the Christians, you **must** do two simple things: set aside all rational thinking. If you think rationally and use that 10% of our brains we humans can only supposedly access, than you cannot find yourself believing in God. Only by setting aside your rational thought can you have faith. If you think critically and rationally and study the basic principles of God, He/She/It cannot exist. The other thing you **must** do is make excuses. You must make excuses on God's behalf to A: justify your faith and go against all rationality, and B: to justify all that is wrong with the conflicts between faith and the brutal reality of life. The excuses ranges from pretty lame to ludicrous, to the outright ignorant, but religious people make them and then push aside all reason to justify and satisfy their delusion.

Let us start with transcendence and omnipresence. Transcendence means that an object or being surpasses the state of physical existence and at the same time is separate from it. Omnipresence means that an object, or being, is unbound and is in all places in space and time at all times. Together these two words signify all material and temporal existence. If a being is transcendent it is outside of time. Rationally we know that is not possible. A being cannot be outside of time, hence it would not exist. A being cannot be omnipresent or else it would occupy all matter within the universe, leaving room for nothing else. A being cannot occupy all matter, time, and space and at the same time be beyond space and time or else it would not exist within the material to occupy all matter; hence being omnipresent is not possible. Confusing, to say the least, but a religious person simply goes with the theory that, "Hey, it's God. He can do anything, be anywhere, and be anything. He is not bound by His own laws, or the laws that the universe follows even though He made those laws." That is not thinking rationally or critically. If you think logically, rationally, and critically, it is painfully obvious that beings do not reside outside of time, nor do they occupy all matter within space and time.

Omnipotence. To be all powerful. The ability to do anything and to defy any law of the universe. The power to subject all of reality, space, time, and material presence to your whims. God is supposed to be an omnipotent being, yet, according to the book of Genesis it took God six days to create all of creation. Then, on the seventh day, God rested. That is omnipotence? Six days to create everything and then a day off? Why not just snap those transcendent fingers and *poof!* Creation! An omnipotent being would not need six days, nor would it need a day to rest. A being that needs to rest is obviously not omnipotent.

"How do you know how long a day was? Before creation there was timelessness. How can we know God's version of time since He is beyond space and time?" Those are the arguments my religious peers always hit me with. I love to answer them and shoot their irrationality full of holes.

Genesis 001:004 *...And God saw the light, that it was good: and God divided the light from the darkness.*

Genesis 001:005 *...And God called the light Day, and the darkness he called Night. And the evening and the morning were the first day.*

According to the bible, in the very first lines of the book, God deemed that from the evening to the morning to be one day, a 24-hour day. This is why Jewish holidays always begin at sundown the night before, as evening begins the cycle. To go against this fundamentally destroys any faith in the God in which people believe. For thousands of years people have dwelled upon the verses above, and have tried to equate and rationalize them.

Poets and astronomers, great thinkers, and clergy alike have all put their spoons in the pot and have debated the meaning of time as set forth by their god. I am none of these, nor am I a wise man or a sage, but I would say this: if you take the bible as the word of God, how dare you try and interpret it any other way than what is written? It states clearly that God deemed one evening to the next morning a day. That is how God measures time. That is how He meant for us to measure time. To even debate the issue shows a lack of faith.

Just for good measure, science has recently shown us that billions of years ago when the earth formed, days were much shorter, almost by half. Another few billion years after the earth formed so, too, did the moon, and it stabilized earth's orbit. The moon also slowed down the spin of earth due to the drag and gravitational tug of the earth's mighty oceans, and days became longer.

"I suggest that the anthropomorphic god-idea is not a harmless infirmity of human thought, but a very noxious fallacy, which is largely responsible for the calamities the world is at present enduring."
William Archer, 1667 – 1735

Moving on but staying with omnipotence, we come to that delightful thing knows as the conundrum. Some say that this next argument is moot and superfluous, but how do you measure God's might? How do you measure omnipotence? Can God create a rock so heavy that He cannot lift, or can He not create such a rock? Is God all powerful and is He the way of light and purity or can He not defeat 'evil' and His counterpart in Satan? Why, if Satan exists, does God allow it and why can He not simply erase Satan from existence? Say what you will of the conundrums, but answer them with a rational answer. It cannot be done. You have to make up some of those excuses on God's behalf to do so. If you do not feel like making excuses, you can always pull the haughty act, and say that those questions are beneath God and not worthy of an answer as to the validity of their nature. That, my friend, is another excuse.

Omniscience is to know everything past, present, and future. Did knowledge exist before God, or did God create knowledge when He made all of creation? Supposing God existed before knowledge there would have been no knowledge whatsoever for God to know making knowledge inaccessible even to God prior to whatever knowledge existed before creation. Whew! A lot of uses of the word "knowledge", but hopefully you get the point. Read it again if you need to.

The bible touts God as transcendent, of being outside space and time. If God is transcendent and omniscient than He would know everything outside of space, time, and creation. He would know of everything that is both in and out of existence at any given time in space/time/history thus making God's mind akin to a hard drive of infinite storage space, but one that cannot delete its own files or have them altered in any way.

Then there are all those gaps—holes that need to be filled with knowledge, the unanswered questions of us, the world, and the universe that dog us every day. There are millions of these gaps. They confound us, perplex us, and confuse us. They keep us awake at night. They make us bite our nails and scratch our heads. The gaps are everywhere. How simple to fill them with a three letter word: God. "I don't know, so it must be God. We have not yet found an answer to this question, so it must be God. Science has not shown us the reason for this phenomenon or this simple action, so it must be God. It is so perplexing and so infinitely creative that mere chance or cosmic coincidence could not have produced this effect so it must be God." God of the Gaps is what this is called, and it really is quite infuriating. Just because mankind has not figured something out does not mean we need to default to God. Since the answer to some cosmic riddle has not been found does not mean we must default to an omnipotent deity. Because something is so simple yet so intricate does not mean there is God. Man's own incredible ego has created this God, and all gods before. Man's own fear of death and nothingness has created religion. Man's own ignorance keeps him in fear of God and blinds him to the plight of our species and the potential we possess.

The God of the Gaps does nothing but hold us back in terms of scientific development as well as true spiritual development. God is a convenient answer for all those questions that we cannot yet answer. It lets our minds deal with the unknown and gives us a simple, easy-to-digest answer. God did it. Simple. Easy. No need to think critically or rationally.

> *"A blessed and indestructible being has no trouble himself and brings no trouble upon any other being; so he is free from anger and partiality, for all such things imply weakness."*
> Epicurus, 341 – 270 BC

So, is there really anybody atop that mountain? If there is, why all the secrecy? Why all the cryptic nonsense? Why all the top-secret agendas? Why not appear, and show us—prove to us—that God is real? Why does the Lord have to work in mysterious ways? Why would a being that is omniscient, omnipotent, and transcendent act in such a fashion? It does not sound very mature to me. Why would such a being even care at all? Why must He be praised constantly? I call that being vain and gloating. "Hey, look what I did. Now thank me for it until the end of time." Would not a being such as God be above all of this, above even us and our praise or condemnation? I know if I were inconceivably, vastly, godly superior to all other life in existence I could and would care less if I was praised, belittled, or ignored. Sticks and stones, after all.

God is an anthropomorphized creation. Ancient man—as in men, the male of our species—put all of his traits into the deity he wanted to worship: Immortal. Wise beyond measure. All powerful. Fearless. Superior to women. Needing of praise and worship. Justifiable war, rape, murder, and hate. There is no such thing as human nature any more, only human behavior, and we put all of those behavioral patterns into the gods we wish to create and then follow as they allow—nay, as they command.

> *"If we go back to the beginnings of things, we shall always find that ignorance and fear created the gods; that imagination, rapture and deception embellished them; that weakness worships them; that custom spares them; and that tyranny favors them in order to profit from the blindness of men."*
> Paul-Henri, Baron d'Holbach, 1723 – 1789

When you think rationally, cognitively, and critically, God cannot exist. God is supposed to be not only omnipotent, omniscient, and transcendent, but He is perfect. If that is the case then what happened during the immeasurable time before creation? If God created all of creation from nothing, what existed before the nothing? There must have been some semblance of constancy. If not, then whatever reality that existed before was imperfect. A perfect being acts perfectly. If there was no constancy, was their boredom? Did God create the universe, and ultimately man, because He was bored? Did He create man to praise and worship Him out of a sense of loneliness? A perfect being could not feel these emotions and certainly would not act upon them. A perfect being has no desires and no such trivial sentiments. It is therefore a conclusion that a perfect being, or God, is paradoxical, and cannot exist.

If we expand this argument and allow for a perfect being such as God to have created the universe, and man, then we must ask *just what was He thinking?* We humans are certainly far from perfect, yet, according to the bible, we are made in God's image. Free will aside, a perfect being (one with omniscience nonetheless) made us, and look how we turned out. Imperfect creations from a perfect creator is another paradox, and hence a perfect creator, or God, cannot exist.

To press the issue, to say we are made in God's image is not saying much at all. The God of Judeo-Christianity is a blood-thirsty tyrant, a jealous, vain entity, and one who is intolerant and spiteful. These are not only my words, but the words used to describe God as in the bible— God's divinely-inspired book. This is nothing to be proud of. I am but a mortal man, an imperfect human. I have only my human brain to rely on, human emotions to call upon, and human experiences to base thing on, but if I were a deity [of a pure and good nature] and for some reason needed lesser beings to surround myself with, praise and adulate me, I would create as follows: I would fashion a universe that was as friendly as it is mysterious. Space and time and the planets would be pretty much as they are now with the exception that stars would not die, flare, or cause havoc, nor would proximity cause problems. I would fashion billions and billions of planets with life that was so varied only a deity such as me could fathom such diversity. Comets and meteors, and other space phenomena would in no way impact life and planetary systems.

I would then create a race of cognitively, consciously intelligent beings. To make it easy for our minds to comprehend, let us call these creations humans. There would be two sexes; male and female. The females would all look like Lucy Lawless (from her Xena days—yes, I have a crush on her, as you can tell by now), Jennifer Aniston, and/or Jada Pinkett-Smith. The males would all look like Antonio Banderas, Denzel Washington, and/or Hugh Jackman. Well, that is not entirely fair, so let us just say that these humans would be varied in looks, hair, skin, and eye color, and all would be gorgeous and physically flawless. They would not be capable of hate, jealously, or anger. They would possess only love, kindness, and decency—and a healthy drive for physical contact and relations. My humans would be truly immortal, as would all of the creatures in my multi-verse; there would be no sickness, no death. There would be no adverse weather on any world, and no need for shelter, clothes, or material needs. No creature, including the humans, would be able to breed (despite any sex drive and sex would be purely an emotion/physical activity for the humans to enjoy). All creatures would eat only vegetables and fruits, and despite any teeth, fangs, spines, or whatnot, there would be no competition for food, and food would only be eaten for amusement and discovery and taste, not for sustenance. The humans would not know war, hate, or evil; such things would simply not exist. Humans would have the power to fly of their own accord, breathe air and water, and could traverse the stars to visit the untold amount of planets. Their bodies would be immutable and resistant—think of everyone's favorite Kryptonian. All humans would have been created with full knowledge of me and would be thankful at their leisure, with no threats of punishment for missing an opportunity to praise their creator. They could even ignore me, never say "thanks", and that would be fine, too. I am, after all, a perfect god, and my feelings cannot be hurt.

28

"God does not play dice with the universe."
Albert Einstein, 1879 – 1955

"Black holes would seem to suggest that God not only plays dice, but also sometimes throws them where they cannot be seen."
Stephen Hawking, 1942 –

"God plays *dice* with the universe, but they're loaded dice."
Joseph Ford, 1927 – 1995

The planets would not be millions of light years apart, but close together so that they could be visited easily, yet not destroy the surrounding region of space due to gravitational proximity. The humans could have eternity to discover the universe in all its varied beauty and splendor—different creatures on a multitude of worlds, alien sunsets and sunrises, oceans, forests, fields, plains, stars, swimming, picking wildflowers, tasting the different fruits and vegetables and such of a billion worlds, feeding birds and watching butterflies, making love, free love/shared love/group love. The people could perfect, if they so wished, forms of the arts; music, painting, expression, theater, dance, poetry… or they could sit on the home planet of Earth and do nothing. They would have true free will.

Perhaps I would create hundreds—thousands—of human-like races, all with different physical traits and art skills, and these multitudes of races could travel about the universe and meet, greet, and share with each other. Call me crazy, but if I were a god that is what I would do for my beloved creations. Look what we have. Is our universe anything remotely like that? Is our universe remotely kind or benevolent? Of course the answer is 'no'. Our universe is blindly apathetic, callous and cold, remorseless and harsh, yet beautiful in its own wonderful way, but not because of anything labeled divine.

"Jesus' last words on the cross, "My God, my God, why hast thou forsaken me?" hardly seem like the words of a man who planned it that way. It doesn't take Sherlock Holmes to figure there is something wrong here."
Donald Morgan, author

Taking the argument even further, we have a perfect creator, God, who sends mankind, His imperfect creation, a flesh-and-blood version of Himself whom He calls His son. This son is allowed to be tortured and murdered for no other reason than man's easily inspired ire. If we add that God is omniscient and knew of these events that would occur before they happened, yet allowed them to occur creates yet another paradox: a perfect creator, God, creating an imperfect version of Himself, Jesus Christ, and allowing imperfect creations, mankind, to slay the imperfect version of God. The paradox is obvious, as is the conclusion; a perfect creator cannot exist.

If God is omniscient as well as transcendent, then nothing in the universe can be hidden from Him. Emotions cannot be hidden from Him. New experiences cannot be hidden from Him, as He would know of everything that has ever or will ever happen. Nothing new can ever be learned by Him. Therefore, there is no need for God to have emotions—nothing can surprise Him, and nothing could make Him elated, nor could anything truly anger Him since He knew it would happen and He *allowed* it to happen. Where is the need for anger at "sinners"? This

paradox shows that an omniscient being that is also omnipotent cannot have human emotions, yet the bible says that God does indeed have emotions, and He feels what humans feel. That is a contradiction, a contrast to the state of omniscience, and a transparent argument. A perfect being, God, who has emotional responses and feelings—even vicariously—is impossible.
I do believe that our mountain climber is out of luck, as the mountain top is most definitely uninhabited.

"The most ridiculous concept ever perpetrated by H. Sapiens is that the Lord God of Creation, Shaper and Ruler of the Universes, wants the saccharine adoration of his creations, that he can be persuaded by their prayers, and becomes petulant if he does not receive this flattery. Yet this ridiculous notion, without one real shred of evidence to bolster it, has gone on to found one of the oldest, largest and least productive industries in history."
Robert A. Heinlein, 1907 - 1988

Five: Is God Love?

Ask any Jewish or Christian person what God is to them and many will answer that God is love, God is kind, and God's ways are those of mercy and compassion, and a path to life ever-lasting. That is what a religious person will tell you. Yet, to modern sensibilities freed from the fear of offense to church or deity, or to the harsh consequences that have historically followed in doing so, the picture of God that emerges in almost every book of the Talmud and New Testament defies any rationale for the above sentiments. From Genesis to the Ten Commandments to Revelations, both Old and New Testaments are rife with murder, slavery, human and animal sacrifice, war, punishment, suffering, rape, genocide, intolerance, and male chauvinism, and all not only ordained by God, but demanded by Him! The Good Book certainly has a good deal of hate-driven violence in it, that is for sure.

I find it comical to the point of irony and hypocrisy the stance the faithful put on life, especially human life. The Catholic Church is one of the largest hypocrites in this category. Look through the Good Book and show me where God puts value on human life? Of all the world's religions the God of Judeo-Christianity ranks as one of the most bloodthirsty, sacrifice-craving gods out there. From a natural standpoint, and a point of fact, most women self-abort nearly half of their pregnancies. This is a natural occurrence that most women do not even know they undergo. This would be "abortion" of sorts, and one set into motion by God Himself. Where is the outcry? Where is the outrage? God puts very little effort into nourishing life, so why do the faithful nourish it? It stands to reason that killing, murder, rape, and all the horrible things we do to one another are wrong on a level that transcends religion. One does not need God, or a god, to tell us what is right and wrong. In fact, gods can only steer us far away from that path, a lesson that history has tried to teach us over and over since the dawn of time, but a lesson mankind has yet to grasp and take to heart.

I believe it to be an irrefutable fact that man wrote the Torah, man wrote the bible, and it is man who has instilled all his own behavioral patterns in his concept of God. If indeed I am wrong we come to an interesting juncture. If God is real, and the Torah and the bible are His words, we are faced with the horrifying truth that God is anything but love, and is nothing short of an omnipotent and transcendent source of all that is considered evil. As verse after verse and book after book of the bible portray God, He is never satisfied. He creates, He destroys, He allows, He does not allow. He kills and punishes on a whim and is capable of mass murder and genocide, and prone to ecological destruction.

If the biblical God is real, and He is the Creator, we *cannot* separate the good from the bad and see only His "good" works. If God created the heavens and the earth, the birds and the bees, man and all the animals, then He also created bacteria, disease, malformations, suffering, evil, lies, sickness, plague, natural disasters (or are they not natural at all and purposeful?). Either God created all or God did not create all. It cannot be separated and excused no matter how you

31

slice up the pie that is "all of creation." Apologists try to do so, or make more excuses, but the fact is that if God is real, then evil, sickness, war, famine, disasters, disease, child death, pedophilia, necrophilia, murder, and all the bad that opposes the good is His idea, His creation, and His fault. It started in Genesis with one of His first creations, Cain. Cain was a jealous murderer, and is man not fashioned in God's likeness?

> *"There is no book which tells of a more infamous monster than the Old Testament, with its Jehovah of murder and cruelty and revenge, unless it be the New Testament, which arms its God with hell, and extends His outrages throughout all eternity!"*
> Helen H. Gardener, 1853 - 1925

Part I: God is not kind, but cruel and harsh. He is apathetic at best.

> *"The usual Christian argument is that the suffering in the world is purification for sin and is therefore a good thing. This argument is, of course, only a rationalization of sadism; but in any case it is a very poor argument. I would invite any Christian to accompany me to the children's ward of a hospital, to watch the suffering that is there being endured, and then to persist in the assertion that those children are so morally abandoned as to deserve what they are suffering. In order to bring himself all feelings of mercy and compassion, he must, in short, make himself as cruel as the God in whom he believes."*
> Bertrand Russell, 1872 – 1970

The suffering of innocent children alone should be enough for us to indict God for his misfeasance toward us—even to the meekest, least blame-worthy "beloved" creations. What more do humans need in order to reject the notion of His heavenly munificence and begin to see God in his all-too human irrationality? If the insurmountable and horrifying ways in which innocent children, who through no fault of their own, go through inconceivable suffering before they die or that they die at all via disease, birth defects, and starvation, then what of this God who so many find loving?

Some branches of Christianity preach that all people are born sinners, that they are born evil and must redeem themselves as they go through life. I find this concept preposterous, and it amazes me that anyone can remain without outrage at this teaching that innocent children are damned at birth simply for being born.

Imagine a newborn child. You hold him or her in your arms and look at this new life. Do you see sin and vice, evil and hate? What possible thing could this newborn have done to be labeled a sinner or evil? Again, if you are a Christian and believe in the tenets of the faith, God made us in His image. Are we saying that God is inherently evil and a sinner? If so that would explain it all, would it not? What possible excuse must one make for God to explain this suffering? What possible reason could a loving, perfect deity have to cause such suffering in innocent, new life? Whatever the excuse is will be a poor, pathetic one at best, but the faithful blindly excuse their God as if the suffering of children (or any one) is some divine mystery best left alone.

One of the trials of life is having the young, especially the newborn, die. Whether by sickness and injury, accidental, or murder, a parent burying a child has to be one of the worst scenarios I can imagine for an adult. In turn, the general attitude represented by anyone of faith for these occasions generally turns my stomach. Time and time again, from people of all denominations of Judeo-Christianity two ever-popular adages creep into the consoling they give: "God bless the child," or even more disturbing is "God must have called that soul home," or "God must have special work for them," or something akin to that sentiment.

My response is: God is supposed to be transcendent, immortal, and infinite, outside of time and space. Time has no meaning to God, and the span of a human life lived to its longest day would not even be a fraction of the blink of an eye to a being such as He. If God, in its omniscient and transcendent state, could not wait for the child to grow up, learn to ride a bike, play some baseball and eat some ice cream, to make friends and go to a prom, to learn about love and laughter, to experience carnal pleasures, to sail a boat and to fly a kite, to marry (or not), to have children (or not), to travel and explore this wonderful world God made for us then that is no god worth worshiping. Only a vain, jealous, impatient god would snuff the life of a child because it wants and needs companionship. Perfect beings do not want and need. Perfect beings of love do not kill. Perfect beings of love can wait since time has no meaning. "God bless that child." Apparently God did not bless that child; the poor thing was run over by a train, or killed by a neighborhood dog, or raped by a low-life scumbag, or died of an incurable disease. Had God blessed the child it would have lived a long, happy life, not a short painful one.

Reflecting its God, the Christian faith is not a code of morals. It is a faith based on salvation and redemption, not of doing what is right by your fellow man. If we are all born with evil and sin in our hearts, our perfect creator made us that way. If I, an anti-theist, am the way I am did not God make me this way? Who are you to question Him in instilling me with such notions?

Why bother with salvation and redemption if a perfect creator created us in His image? Who are we to mess with what God has created? Perhaps He wants us evil and to be sinners; why else would he have made us in His image? Perhaps only the evil person and the sinner get to go to Heaven? Maybe it is the non-believer who shows the strength, courage, and conviction to deny God that gets into Heaven because God wants only the strong of heart and people true to themselves to surround Him. Then again, if God is perfect what need does he have to be surrounded by such lesser beings? Humans want people around out of loneliness, a very human emotion, something a perfect being would not experience. I am the furthest thing from perfect, and I do not want people around me all day. I need "me" time. If were immortal and transcendent my attitude would be "bugger off. Leave me alone. Beat it, kid, or I'll hit you with a bag of nickels." Instead of pulling the wings off of flies I'd do it to angels if they kept singing praises and fluttering about me all day and night.

At best, the Judeo-Christian God is one of apathy. Even a fleeting glance of human history will show the amount of war, strife, and bloodshed that stains us. Whether the killing was done for money or gold, or for land and territory, or in the name of the gods—including God— there has not been a single day since mankind appeared that has not been marred by man-made death and destruction. Add "Acts of God"—natural disasters—into the mix and things become more interesting to consider in terms of God's callousness toward us, His greatest and beloved creations.

Was it not a few scant years back in 2005 when hurricane Katrina slammed into Louisiana, killing thousands of people and destroying the city which has yet to bounce back financially, emotionally, and ecologically? After the devastation, Pastor John Hagee said of the storm:*"Hurricane Katrina was, in fact, the judgment of God against the city of New Orleans.*

New Orleans had a level of sin that was offensive to God. There was to be a homosexual parade there on the Monday that the Katrina came."

As I write this in the month of May, 2008, an earthquake in China killed tens of thousands the same week a cyclone in Burma killed close to another hundred thousand. That same week tornados ripped through the central United States killing only a dozen or so, but they killed none the less. This is just the tip of the iceberg of nature's wrath in that past month. How many natural disasters throughout the ages have killed innocent people? If God is the creator, and God either created the weather patterns or controls them directly, He is responsible. He may have given man free will, but is Mother Nature a separate entity with free will of Her own? Highly unlikely. Are we saying that every person who dies as a result of natural disasters is a sinner, and not a single one among them is a 'saved' person? Highly unlikely.

Nature's wrath is another way of saying acts of God, but both cast blame on God, yet He goes on with mankind absolving this behavior. The truth is that nature kills indiscriminately: rich, poor, old, young, black, white, Asian, sick, healthy, Jew, Christian, Mormon, Muslim, and so on. God is indistinguishable from nature, and so ultimately God must be held responsible for any deaths in this fashion. This bubble of delusion is easily popped when you realize that God does not exist, and nature kills without rhyme or reason, without malice or intent.

Natural forces are affected by action and reaction, just like everything in the universe. The earth heats and cools in cycles. Ice ages come and go on this planet as a natural function as affected by the planet's axis, it weather patterns, the salinity of the oceans, and our orbit and relation to the sun.

If God does exist, His apathy does not end with natural disasters. Let us take adult suffering and measure that. Throughout the ages, how many devoutly religious blind, deaf, and amputees have never been divinely cured? Aside from stories in the bible where Jesus cured one man of blindness (why not cure them all and eradicate the condition?) I see no evidence of the blind praying for sight and receiving it. No, Benny Hinn and his ilk do not count. Let me see if I can recall ever having heard of an amputee—or even a person born with missing limbs—having prayed for restored health and received it. I cannot do so, nor can I research one case. Does God dislike amputees? Does He harbor ill will toward the deaf and the blind? A perfect, loving deity would not harbor any such resentment, nor would a perfect being create such imperfect creatures in its own image. Why would God completely ignore an amputee? For the same reason the prayers of cancer patients, blind people, diabetics, deaf people, and all the people with their various illnesses and diseases are ignored: God does not exist.

Apologists and the faithful can proselytize and write books upon books all they like, but the blatant truth is that prayer is not real. Prayer is a delusion. Mind over matter (to an extent) is one thing, and the power of positive thinking is another, but prayer is only faith. Prayer is not real, just a fancy name for a daydream, a wish upon a star. Not one person in the history of the world has come back from death due to prayer. Prayer does not cure illness, or allow you to win the lottery, or get you that fancy sports car. Hard work gets you that car. A body's immune system, with the aid of medical professionals and modern medicine, cures diseases and illness if the conditions are correct. If God were real, and prayer real, and since the faithful certainly outnumber the non-faithful, why, then, are there hospitals? Why are there still disease and sickness, birth defects and the need for doctors and surgeons?

"Two hands working can do more than a thousand clasped in prayer."
Anonymous

34

I recall last year in 2007-8, when the state of Georgia was going through a long-lasting drought. On the news I heard that the mayor was calling people to go to the town square to have a pray-in. They were going to get together and pray to God for rain. It was obvious to me that, if God was real, then He knew there was a drought in Georgia. In fact, He was responsible for it. As such, what good would praying for rain be if the God who you are begging for rain from is the same omniscient, omnipotent God that is withholding the rain? It is backwards thinking from delusional people.

Now, as I write this book, there is massive flooding in the state of Iowa. One hundred city blocks have flooded, power has been disrupted, homes lost, and lives turned upside down. From the Associated Press comes the following tidbit:

"We're just kind of at God's mercy right now, so hopefully people that never prayed before this, it might be a good time to start," Linn County Sheriff Don Zeller said. "We're going to need a lot of prayers and people are going to need a lot of patience and understanding."

Let me get this straight. You are going to pray to God, the same god who has you by the small hairs? You will pray for what, exactly? It is apparent that this deity does not care one iota for you in Iowa, yet you will pray for the flood waters to recede? As with the people in Georgia, what sort of nonsense is this? Natural disasters are natural. Praying is akin to doing nothing. The power of prayer is fictional, while hard work and relief efforts are tangible. The god you pray to, by the way, is the same god that flooded your city—if you believe in God, you take the good with the bad and it cannot be separated.

For millions upon millions of years the weather patterns have not changed. We know that the United States was once part of the super-continent known as Pangaea. Since its split from the super land mass, the U.S. has retained much of its shape and continuity. Texas, Louisiana, Mexico, and the rest of the Gulf Coast have been hit with an untold number of hurricanes, and will for as long as the North and South American continents remain as they are. If you are a person of faith, why is this area so inclined to hurricanes? Despite the natural reasons stemming from a hurricane's birth out on the warm, tropical seas to the winds and currents that drive them westward toward our country, what would a deity continually have against that part of the world? For that matter, why is the Midwest U.S. plagued with tornadoes and thunderstorms, flooding, and hail? It seems to reason that since this area of the United Sates—also known as the Bible Belt, home to more devout Christians than anywhere in the country—has more religious people that it would be less likely a target for such natural disasters….but no. This region of the North American continent suffers more hurricanes, more tornadoes, and more rain storms that cause flood, hail, and lightning strikes than any other part of the States. Again, would it not be the other way around, since God is loyal to His faithful? It only makes sense when it is realized that nature and God are not the same; nature does what it is programmed to do (by the natural laws of the universe, which is simply organized chaos) regardless of human faith and kills indiscriminately, and that God is not existent.

It is now late September, 2008, and as I edit and pour over my own work, a hurricane of great strength has already hit Louisiana…yet again. Hurricane Gustav just ripped through the region, decimating the lives of thousands of people, especially in Cuba. Now, only a week after Gustav, Hurricane Ike is aiming right for the area Gustav hit. Lightning can strike the same place twice. From the A.P.:

"The first one left me something, but this one left me nothing," said Olga Atiaga, a 53-year-old housewife. Gustav obliterated her roof and some walls. Then Ike blew away a mattress and smashed the kitchen sink. "I don't even have anything to sleep on," she said.

"We repaired the roof two days ago and this one took the new one," she said. "I'm ready to move to Canada! We have spent eight days drying out things, cleaning everything, sleeping on the floor, and now we are hit again." says Odalis Cruz, a 45-year-old housing inspector.

"....21-year-old Niyel Rodriguez she had to move to a shelter with her 19-day-old daughter Chanel. She huddled Tuesday with 109 expectant and new mothers and their children in a wing of an Old Havana maternity hospital."

Is this a demonstration of How God is kind and caring, of how He loves us, His most favored of creations? No, this is a demonstration of nature's power and unabashed neutrality in how it offers beauty and life with one hand and destroys and kills with the other. Storm after storm, the weather is the most formidable force on this planet. We live and die by nature's whims, and luckily for us nature has no agenda. Life will find a way, as always, but no one said it had to be easy. Natural cause and action, action and reaction, and sentient/cognitive decisions made by all living things govern every happenstance in the universe, not gods and/or celestial beings playing cosmic chess with us lesser beings. When people realize that sometimes, when shit happens, it is beyond our control, but not some divine mystery. It just is what it is, and that knowledge is somewhat liberating.

*"The President of the United States summons the nation to church on Thanksgiving Day to give thanks to "Almighty God" for the abundant harvest and all other blessings. But what has Almighty God -- I have no desire to appear irreverent -- what has Almighty God as a personal being to do with the harvests? If it is he who produces our crops, then being Almighty there should never be a failure of crops. But since crops frequently fail, it follows that there is no Almighty person in charge of them -- unless he brings failure purposely. Therefore, if God is to be thanked for large crops, he must be blamed when the crops are a failure. . . . If God sends the rain and the sunshine which develops and ripens our wheat, who sends the storms and the insects which destroy much of it? And if he sends both, then why not thank him for one and blame him for the other?"*John Dietrich, 1878 - 1957

Another line right from the bible I love to quote is found in Exodus 33. Here we have Moses leading the exodus out of Egypt. Six hundred thousand fleeing people—all of God's 'chosen' people, ones created by a perfect being—who not only have to worry about Egyptians, but the god that has set them free. Exodus 33:3 "I will send an angel before you and drive out the Canaanites, Amorites, Hittites, Perizzites, Hivites and Jebusites. Go up to the land flowing with milk and honey. But I will not go with you, because you are a stiff-necked people and I might destroy you on the way."

God 'might' destroy you on the way? That is very disheartening. God has set His chosen people free via plague and murder; He will send an angel to kill more of His own creations (the Hittites, Perizzites, etc…) to clear a path for the fleeing chosen people, but they are stubborn and so He may smite them anyway. **This is clearly not a benevolent being, let alone one who is omniscient.** If anything it shows what a bad judge of character God is, how many mistakes He (a perfect being) makes, and how much He likes to kill. You could compare God to Two-Face from the Batman comics—a flip of the coin. Who lives, and who dies?

"God kills indiscriminately, and so shall we. For no creatures under God are as we are, none so like him as ourselves," was what Anne Rice's fictional vampire, Lestat de Lioncourt, said of God. The vampires of myth and legend feed on blood. The vampire that is God feeds on praise and fear and is never sated. God is easily displeased by His own creations, and arbitrarily decided to favor one group of humans over another based on what….real estate and point of origin? This is not tolerance, but hatred and xenophobia.

The God of the Torah and the Bible cares only for what people believe, not what they do. For this Supreme Being, your actions do not speak louder that your spoken (or unspoken) words. His skin is so thin that any affront to His ego warrants eternal punishment, but acts of hate, violence, genocide, and intolerance are perfectly acceptable so long as you "believe in Him". Let us not forget the special intolerance God seems to have for women as they suffer under God's loving care. Starting right in Genesis, God takes an instant hate on women. Because Eve ate from the forbidden tree, she and all future women were punished with great pains and suffering during childbirth. Supposedly Eve was born able to birth young with no adverse effects. After eating an apple, however, this was not to be so. Furthermore there are numerous passages in the torah and bible which state that women who are not virgins upon their wedding night are to be killed, and that women that are raped should be killed, and so on. To be fair the bible tells us to kill not only the raped but the rapist as well, but what if a woman willingly has sex with a man before her marriage? She is to be stoned to death, but the man walks Scott free? Seems one-sided, no? It shows that man wrote the bible and was inspired by his own wants, not any divine love or kindness.

"A God who could make good children as easily a bad, yet preferred to make bad ones; who could have made every one of them happy, yet never made a single happy one; who made them prize their bitter life, yet stingily cut it short; who gave his angels eternal happiness unearned, yet required his other children to earn it; who gave is angels painless lives, yet cursed his other children with biting miseries and maladies of mind and body; who mouths justice, and invented hell -- mouths mercy, and invented hell -- mouths Golden Rules and forgiveness multiplied by seventy times seven, and invented hell; who mouths morals to other people, and has none himself; who frowns upon crimes, yet commits them all; who created man without invitation, then tries to shuffle the responsibility for man's acts upon man, instead of honorably placing it where it belongs, upon himself; and finally, with altogether divine obtuseness, invites his poor abused slave to worship him!
Mark Twain, 1835 - 1910

This next example was something I had originally put in this book, took out, and decided to put back in. This past spring I was driving my son to school, and on the way home I was behind a pickup truck. I live in a small town; not country and not city, and traffic in the spring here is next to nothing on our winding, semi-country roads. As I drove home, a squirrel darted out into the road and was struck by the pickup. I saw it happen, knew it was too late for the rodent, but winced anyway. I was about 3 car-lengths behind that truck with not a car behind me. I felt horrible for the squirrel, but what was worse was that the strike did not kill the animal outright. It must have caught a glancing blow that crushed some part of the animal, for when I looked in my rear-view mirror, I could see the poor thing rolling, flopping, and arcing into the air a few feet, only to impact back onto the pavement. It was in obvious agony—perhaps its legs were crushed, or its hips, or part of its back. It was a wrenching sight, and is still fresh in my mind months after it happened. Call me a sap, but I hate seeing innocent life suffer so, be it human or animal. Nature and the food chain is one thing, but....

As soon as it happened my anti-theist mind went into action, and thought that if the god of Judeo-Christianity *is* real and *is* omnipotent and transcendent, why would It allow such a folly? What, in Its benevolent, all-seeing mind was going on? Are squirrels born sinners? Do animals not garner God's mercy? What possible reason would God, who knows all, sees all, and plans all, have to send such suffering to that squirrel? The reason was clear, and plain as day; God does not exist, and the universe is apathetic and blind to life and the struggles and plights of all living things. The only other answer is that God is real, and is truly cruel and callous, but I am banking on the first option.

You, too, can see the evidence of cruel apathy at work. Just drive down the street. I live in a semi-rural area in Massachusetts. I cannot drive to the store, to the mall, or to the city without seeing bodies lining the sides of the streets: squirrels, skunks, opossums, raccoons, birds, cats, or moles. They all lay upon the sides of the roads, crushed and bloodied, the crows having a fresh feast each day. Is this what God had intended? Are these animals so worthless that they deserve to be killed by the dozens each day? Or is God jealous of these superior creations? Animals do not need technology, manufactured weapons, clothing, nor do they need war or hate. Animals are more resilient to harm, to the elements, to disease and sickness. They are much more agile than and many times as strong as humans (in comparison to almost all living things, humans rank among the physically weakest, most sense-deprived, most disease and sickness-prone, and least-agile species on the planet). Since God did not instill a soul in animals, does that make them worthless of being nothing better than road kill?

Moving away from apathy let us see how loving and kind God is. To do so we shall take examples right out of scripture, from the Torah and the bible.

> *"Atheism leaves a man to sense, to philosophy, to natural piety, to laws, to reputation; all of which may be guides to an outward moral virtue, even if religion vanished; but religious superstition dismounts all these and erects an absolute monarchy in the minds of men."*
> Francis Bacon, 1561 – 1626

Part II: God is Bloodthirsty

Many of God's defenders argue that without God there are no morals, and that the greatest evils come from men and regimes that were atheistic. Christianity's defenders will dredge up names like Stalin, Hitler, Pol Pot, Kim Ill Jong, and the other usual suspects. Defenders will extol that these men and their atheist regimes killed millions of people, and caused/cause untold suffering. What the defenders miss, of course, is the big picture: God is the biggest mass-murderer of all time. Between His edicts, His demands, His flood, His rage-fueled massacres, God has Himself been the cause of death of untold millions—this is, of course, looking at it from an outside view. I am not saying that God is real, but taking stock of the situation and saying if God is real, He has more to account for than all the men above and then some….and He is supposed to be the source of peace, goodness, righteousness, and love?

Another point of view is that of all the peoples of the world, the ancient Jews were to be the "chosen" ones. Does that really make any sense? Let us just pretend that the story of Genesis is real, and Adam and Eve's descendents really did populate the world. All of these people would be God's children, but God seems to favor one tribe over all the others. There are so many lines and verses in the Torah of how God gives the go ahead—in some cases the outright command—for his favored tribe to war with and eradicate the others. Now, millennia later, many Jews still claim to be God's chosen people, and point out that even after all the things their people have been through that they are still here. Despite the Roman conquest and subjugation of the Holy Land, the Inquisition, and the Holocaust, these believers hold on to that claim. I would go the opposite route and argue that how can any people claim to be the chosen people of a celestial deity when so many atrocities have happened to them over the eons?

During the time in which the Torah was written, cultural anthropology teaches us that violence and death were part of everyday life. The Sumerian and Assyrian people were a warrior people at heart, and so were the deities to which they prayed. When the Assyrians, Sumerian, and Egyptians (and other) cultures were assimilated and reworked by the people who became the Hebrews, they kept the penchant for bloodthirsty, demanding deity worship. This is more than evident than as written in the Torah.

Within these two holy texts are the numerous demands and commands from God to kill, murder, and sacrifice both humans and animals. According to scripture, God punishes King David for the sole act of taking a census. For that act God created a pestilence that killed 70,000 people which can be found in 1 Chronicles 21. Call me slow, but does that not go against the very commandment that God decreed? I recall *Thou shall not kill,* or as some translate it, *Thou shall not murder,* as one of the foremost important commandments. Yet look at these passages from the Torah and New Testament:

Exodus 31:12-15 "Then the LORD said to Moses, "Say to the Israelites, 'You must observe my Sabbaths. This will be a sign between me and you for the generations to come, so you may know that I am the LORD, who makes you holy. "Observe the Sabbath, because it is holy to you. Anyone who desecrates it must be put to death." Translation: *Kill people that work on the wrong day of the week.*

Deuteronomy 17:12 "And the man that will do presumptuously, and will not hearken unto the priest that standeth to minister there before the LORD thy God, or unto the judge, even that man shall die: and thou shalt put away the evil from Israel." Translation: *Kill anyone who does not listen to their priest.*

Leviticus 20:13 "If a man lies with a man as one lies with a woman, both of them have done what is detestable. They must be put to death; their blood will be on their own heads." Translation: *Kill all homosexuals.*

Deuteronomy 22:20 "If, however, the charge is true and no proof of the girl's virginity can be found, she shall be brought to the door of her father's house and there the men of her town shall stone her to death. She has done a disgraceful thing in Israel by being promiscuous while still in her father's house. You must purge the evil from among you. "If a man is found sleeping with another man's wife, both the man who slept with her and the woman must die. You must purge the evil from Israel." Translation: *Kill all women who are not virgins. Kill anyone committing adultery.*

Deuteronomy 13: 1-18 "If your very own brother, or your son or daughter, or the wife you love, or your closest friend secretly entices you, saying, "Let us go and worship other gods" (gods that neither you nor your fathers have known, gods of the peoples around you, whether near or far, from one end of the land to the other), do not yield to him or listen to him. Show him no pity. Do not spare him or shield him. You must certainly put him to death. Your hand must be the first in putting him to death, and then the hands of all the people. Stone him to death, because he tried to turn you away from the LORD your God, who brought you out of Egypt, out of the land of slavery. Then all Israel will hear and be afraid, and no one among you will do such an evil thing again. If you hear it said about one of the towns the LORD your God is giving you to live in that wicked men have arisen among you and have led the people of their town astray, saying, "Let us go and worship other gods" (gods you have not known), then you must inquire, probe and investigate it thoroughly. And if it is true and it has been proved that this detestable thing has been done among you, you must certainly put to the sword all who live in that town. Destroy it completely, both its people and its livestock. Gather all the plunder of the town into the middle of the public square and completely burn the town and all its plunder as a whole burnt offering to the LORD your God. It is to remain a ruin forever, never to be rebuilt. None of those condemned things shall be found in your hands, so that the LORD will turn from his fierce anger; he will show you mercy, have compassion on you, and increase your numbers, as he promised on oath to your forefathers, because you obey the LORD your God, keeping all his commands that I am giving you today and doing what is right in his eyes. Translation: *If someone worships another god, kill them. Matter of fact, I command you to kill everyone in a village who worships another god. Kill them with no pity or mercy, burn and raze the village, plunder it and then I might be pleased.*

It is offensive to me that a loving, divine being would mandate that people be killed in his name, but it is evident that this God is not loving. Should you wish to visit more phrases of killing and murder please read the following verses. There are many more than just these and this is just a taste of the professed love God shows us, His chosen and prized creations.

- 2 Kings 11:17, *kill all priests of other religions.*
- 2 Chronicles 15:10 and Exodus 22:19, *kill anyone who does not "seek" or believe in the God of Israel, man and woman alike.* Sounds like another middle-eastern faith everyone condemns.
- Leviticus 24:10, *death for blasphemy.*
- Numbers 1:48, *death to all who approach the Tabernacle.*
- 2 Kings 2:23, *kill bratty children (see the Gospels banned from the Bible, the one that notes Jesus' childhood and was omitted because He was seen as a bratty child).*
- Deuteronomy 20, *the laws of rape.*
- Exodus 22:17, *kill witches/sorceresses.*
- Deuteronomy 22:23-24, *a woman who is raped (and her attacker) must both be put to death.*
- Leviticus 21:9, *burn to death the daughter of a priest who has sex.*
- Exodus 21:15, *kill anyone who hits their father.*
- Leviticus 24:10-16, *kill all blasphemers.*
- Isaiah 14:21, *kill sons for the sins of their fathers.*
- Jeremiah 51:20-26, *commit genocide upon the Babylonians.*

- Leviticus 20:27, *kill all fortunetellers/seers. What then of the prophets—are they not seers?*
- Proverbs 20:20 and Leviticus 20:9, *kill anyone cursing their parents.*
- Kings 2:23-24 God *"slaughters" 50,007men for being curious and peeking into the ark.*

I can choose dozens more passage that show how God not only breaks His own commandments, but demands that the people that are supposed to follow Him break the very commandments He is telling them not to break. Is this a divine case of "do as I say, not as I do"? It cannot be, for God does say to do all this killing. It is a vicious, ridiculous circle. To be redundant, this is a perfect being? This God shows love? This is how a perfect being acts? If this dose of reality does not break the bubble of delusion then we must go on, and further explore the atrocities in the holy scriptures as dictated and inspired by God. If power corrupts, and absolute power corrupts absolutely, where does that leave God? An old argument, yes, but have we a decent answer for it? I would have to say that the answer is this: the God of Judeo-Christianity is absolutely corrupt, yet excused from His actions.

"Isn't killing people in the name of God a pretty good definition of insanity?"
Sir Arthur C. Clarke, 1917 - 2008

Part III: God and Ritual Sacrifice

The God of the Torah and the bible has a thing for burnt offerings. This deity of love and peace seems to enjoy having animals, men, women, and even children killed in His name, and then burnt. Genesis 22:1-18 "Some time later God tested Abraham. He said to him, "Abraham!" "Here I am," he replied. "Then God said, "Take your son, your only son, Isaac, whom you love, and go to the region of Moriah. Sacrifice him there as a burnt offering on one of the mountains I will tell you about." If God is perfect, and is omniscient and knows everything that has and will happen in the past, present, and future, why would God need to test Abraham? Despite the fact that the test involves infanticide and the subsequent immolation of the child's corpse, would not an all-seeing and all-knowing deity simply know what is in Abraham's heart? Would not the conclusion to the test already be known? If not, and Abraham must be tested, then God is neither perfect nor omniscient.

Another example can be found in Judges 11:29-40 "Then the Spirit of the LORD came upon Jephthah. He crossed Gilead and Manasseh, passed through Mizpah of Gilead, and from there he advanced against the Ammonites. And Jephthah made a vow to the LORD : "If you give the Ammonites into my hands, whatever comes out of the door of my house to meet me when I return in triumph from the Ammonites will be the LORD's, and I will sacrifice it as a burnt offering." Then Jephthah went over to fight the Ammonites, and the LORD gave them into his hands. He devastated twenty towns from Aroer to the vicinity of Minnith, as far as Abel Keramim. Thus Israel subdued Ammon. When Jephthah returned to his home in Mizpah, who should come out to meet him but his daughter, dancing to the sound of tambourines! She was an only child. Except for her he had neither son nor daughter. When he saw her, he tore his clothes and cried, "Oh! My daughter! You have made me miserable and wretched, because I have made a vow to the LORD that I cannot break." "My father," she replied, "you have given your word to the LORD. Do to me just as you promised, now that the LORD has avenged you of your enemies, the Ammonites. But grant me this one request," she said. "Give me two months to roam the hills and weep with my friends, because I will never marry." "You may go," he said. And he let her go for two months. She and the girls went into the hills and wept because she would never marry. After the two months, she returned to her father and he did to her as he had vowed. And she was a virgin. Translation: *A warrior asks God for aid in battle, so that he may kill more people. God agrees to lend a hand, but at the cost of a life. It turns out that the offer will be the warrior's own daughter, but that does not stop the warrior or God, and the girl is killed and burned by her own father.*

Again, an omniscient being would know the outcome, and would know if He did lend a cosmic that in the battle that the man's own daughter would be killed. This being of love allows it to take place anyway. There are more passages that deal with human and animal sacrifice, most as burnt offerings. The offerings were burnt so God cold smell them. Going back to omniscience, one would think that God knows (before, during, and after) what or who is being killed as an offering. Why would He need to smell the burning flesh, and why would He need proof? The reason, my dear Watson, is that God does not exist, and the behavioral patterns of ancient men were anthropomorphized into the figure of God. Men needed to smell the burnt offerings. It is possible that at that time in history, the smell of burning flesh—human or animal—excited the senses and men used it as some primal form of satisfaction. Just as a dog rolls in its prey, or a cat or killer whale plays with its victim, early man may have enjoyed the sight and smell of a burning, conquered subject. That concept was put into the god they created.

> *"If we believe absurdities, we shall commit atrocities."*
> Voltaire, 1694 – 1778

Part IV: The Promotion and Rules of Slavery

Many religious apologists will tell you how, without Christianity the world would know no values. They will argue that morals come from Jesus, and ultimately God. Despite that mankind as a species has had thousands of years of social development, all our modern-day morals and values have come only because of Christianity, or so many apologists have said. Slavery, in particular, Christian apologists claim, is something that Christianity brought an end. Almost every early society practiced slavery, such as the Hebrews, Persians, Romans, Egyptians, and even the "enlightened" Greeks. We can plainly see what value human life Judeo-Christianity has in just the few examples we see above. What is more disturbing is that the Judeo-Christian bible asserts a continuation of pre-Christian lack of respect for human life as set forth by God.

There is worse. The bible is a guidebook for slavery and rape. You would think that, as the defenders of Christian values and morals continuously say, Christianity put an end to slavery. It does not, and even Jesus tells people how to keep, manage, and properly beat slaves. It makes you wonder if any of these people have really read the book they hold so dear. If they have read it, did they conveniently forget all the bad things? The southerners in America's Civil War used the bible to promote slavery, and to defend its practice.

Let us see how Christianity champions the anti-slavery movement. To be fair to the religion, the following views are ancient, dating back two millennia. Life then was much, much different than it is now, and modern-day sensibilities and value on human life is much different than it once was. My argument, however, is that the basis for Christian morals is their bible, seen as the "word of God" and a foundation and influence for a code of morals, value, and what is "good". Be that as it may, such sentiments are nowhere to be found in the bible. I argue that modern-day values, morals, and what is "good" comes from human compassion, human cognitive thinking, and from human emotional response. It does not take a book, a religion, or a deity to tell right from wrong.

Deuteronomy 20: 10-15 "When you march up to attack a city, make its people an offer of peace. If they accept and open their gates, all the people in it shall be subject to forced labor and shall work for you. If they refuse to make peace and they engage you in battle, lay siege to that city. When the LORD your God delivers it into your hand, put to the sword all the men in it. As for the women, the children, the livestock and everything else in the city, you may take these as plunder for yourselves. And you may use the plunder the LORD your God gives you from your enemies. This is how you are to treat all the cities that are at a distance from you and do not belong to the nations nearby." Translation: *When you go to war, I, God, approve that you may kill every male left alive. Then you may pillage and plunder like some pirate or Norse warrior. Women, children, and animals are all "prizes" and you can use them as you see fit. In other words, men, have fun. Rape and murder away, and it is alright by Me. Murder children! Forced slavery! Rape! Women are to be treated like animals!*

Exodus 21:7 "If a man sells his daughter as a servant, she is not to go free as menservants do. If she does not please the master who has selected her for himself, he must let her be redeemed. He has no right to sell her to foreigners, because he has broken faith with her. If he selects her for his son, he must grant her the rights of a daughter. If he marries another woman, he must not deprive the first one of her food, clothing and marital rights. If he does not provide her with these three things, she is to go free, without any payment of money." Translation: *Selling your daughter to be a slave is ok. A man may have as many female sex slaves as he wishes, so long as he is able to clothe and feed them. He can force himself upon her year after year and then one day stop feeding her and she can leave, but she gets no payment for her trials.*

In both Exodus:21 and Leviticus:25 we learn that slavery is legal and warranted. These verses explain how and who can be bought and sold, how they are to be treated, and how to beat them properly. If Christianity is the great religion it claims to be, why does it not refute slavery? You would think it would, but in the New Testament Jesus Himself promotes not only slavery, but the beating of slaves. This from the Great Teacher? This from a perfect God who made Himself flesh?

Ephesians 6:5 "Slaves, obey your earthly masters with respect and fear, and with sincerity of heart, just as you would obey Christ. Obey them not only to win their favor when their eye is on you, but like slaves of Christ, doing the will of God from your heart. Serve wholeheartedly, as if you were serving the Lord, not men, because you know that the Lord will reward everyone for whatever good he does, whether he is slave or free."

Luke 12:47 "That servant who knows his master's will and does not get ready or does not do what his master wants will be beaten with many blows. But the one who does not know and does things deserving punishment will be beaten with few blows. From everyone who has been given much, much will be demanded; and from the one who has been entrusted with much, much more will be asked."

"People have suffered and become insane for centuries by the thought of eternal punishment after death. Wouldn't it be better to depend on blind matter than by a god who puts out traps for people, invites them to sin, and allows them to sin and commit crimes he could prevent. Only to

finally get the barbarian pleasure to punish them in an excessive way, of no use for Himself, without them changing their ways and without their example preventing others from committing crimes."
Paul-Henri Thiry baron d'Holbach, 1723 - 1789

We see above that Christianity is no champion of peoples' rights. Believing in the values and tenets of slavery seems to be part of both the Jewish and Christian religions, not to mention the way slavery and rape is to be committed. In Deuteronomy 20, 21, and 22 you can even find the rules and regulations of rape. In other sections, like Numbers: 31, Kings: 9, and Deuteronomy: 3 we learn how the rules of taking spoils of war and how to plunder cities. The next time someone remarks to you that God is Love, or how God and Jesus are the path of righteousness and peace, or how Judeo-Christianity is such a lovely religion, you have some ammunition with which to fight back. If this is love then I would shudder to see hate.

I will end this chapter with a verse from the scriptures. It is taken from the book of Samuel, and is about God punishing King David for taking a Hittite wife. God then forces all the other wives (yes, polygamy was not a punishable act) to be raped multiple times in front of the entire town by willing men. Then the child born to David and the Hittite is killed by God Himself.

Samuel:10 "Now therefore the sword shall never depart from thine house; because thou hast despised me, and hast taken the wife of Uriah the Hittite to be thy wife. Thus saith the LORD, Behold, I will raise up evil against thee out of thine own house, and I will take thy wives before thine eyes, and give them unto thy neighbour, and he shall lie with thy wives in the sight of this sun. For thou didst it secretly: but I will do this thing before all Israel, and before the sun. And David said unto Nathan, I have sinned against the LORD. And Nathan said unto David, The LORD also hath put away thy sin; thou shalt not die. Howbeit, because by this deed thou hast given great occasion to the enemies of the LORD to blaspheme, the child also that is born unto thee shall surely die. And Nathan departed unto his house. And the LORD struck the child that Uriah's wife bare unto David, and it was very sick. David therefore besought God for the child; and David fasted, and went in, and lay all night upon the earth. And the elders of his house arose, and went to him, to raise him up from the earth: but he would not, neither did he eat bread with them. And it came to pass on the seventh day, that the child died."

Does not God command women who are raped *and* their rapists to be put to death? Yes, according to the bible that is to be the outcome of rape, but neither God nor anyone else seems fit to apply this law in the story of David.

"Question with boldness even the existence of a God; because, if there be one, he must more approve of the homage of reason, than that of blind-folded fear."
Thomas Jefferson, 1743 – 1826. 3rd President of the United States

Six: Here Comes the Son

Part 1

Jesus Christ, born of a virgin on December 25th, in the approximate year of 1 to 4 BC. A bright star in the sky announced His arrival, and led three kings to greet the child and welcome Him with gifts. Jesus grew up to be a Rabbi, a teacher, a traveling man who preformed miracles along with his twelve disciples. Jesus was the messiah, the Light of the World, the great redeemer, the Son of God, and known as the Lamb of God. He was killed, buried for three days in a tomb, and then was divinely resurrected, and ascended into Heaven. Most of the civilized world knows the story, even if they are not Christians. Please allow me to tell you another story.

Mithra of Persia, born of a virgin (in this case the Sun) on December 25th. The stars aligned in Orion's belt to signify Mithra's arrival. Mithra grew to be a teacher, and a traveling man who preformed miracles along with his twelve companions. Mithra was the Sun itself, the Light of the World, the God of the Sun, the great redeemer, also known as the Good Sheppard and the Lamb of God. When he died he was placed in a tomb, but was divinely resurrected after three days and ascended into the heavens.

Does the story of the god Mithra sound familiar? I'm not sure . . . I can't place my finger on it, but it does ring some bells. Wait... oh, yes. It sounds similar to that of Jesus Christ, but also reminiscent of another.

Attis of Phrygia (modern day Turkey), a god of vegetation and crops, was born to the virgin, Cybele, on December 25th . He Was called the "Son Divine". He was the redeemer of mankind, and was killed, hung from a tree where his blood dripped down to replenish and redeem the Earth and mankind's sins. He was resurrected three days later on March 25th. Hmmm, sounds a bit familiar, eh? Maybe because this story was brought to Rome more than two-hundred years before the story of Jesus came about. But Attis's story sounds familiar, akin to another one.

Horus, the Egyptian god of the Sky, the Sun and Moon, and of Hunting, was born to the goddess Isis via immaculate conception. Egyptian mythology gives us three dates for His birth, and one is December 25th. He had four followers who followed Him as a youth while He preformed miracles. Horus was killed, torn to pieces and thrown into the Nile where Isis had a crocodile fish out the pieces to resurrect him after a few days. Also note that Isis had a term with which She was adorned, and that term was Meri, the Egyptian word for 'beloved'. It is pronounced Mer-ri. It sounds a lot like Mary, does it not? Again, this story is thousands of years older than the Jesus myth. But Horus and Attis remind me of yet another story...

Dionysus, born of a human woman (Dionysus was conceived divinely) on December 25th and sired by Zeus, King of the Greek gods. Dionysus was the God of Wine. The goddess Hera had the Titans kill Dionysus, but he was resurrected by Zeus and was placed under his protection so that he could no longer be killed. He then traveled around as a teacher and roamed with a small mass of followers to spread the joy of his worship, and preformed miracles along the way.

Dionysus became one of the most important gods of the Greek pantheon, and was an every-day god, and a common household patron.

The big difference between Dionysus and Mihtra to Jesus Christ is that both Mithra and Dionysus predate Jesus by many, many years; Dionysus by a few thousand years, and Mithra by six hundred years. While Dionysus and Jesus share some traits, it is staggering just how much Jesus and Mithra have in common.

The Christian religion is almost identical to the pagan worship of Mithra. There is not one relevant part of the elements that define Christianity from Mithraic tradition. Mithraic cults flourished all over Persia, Greece, Rome, Egypt, parts of ancient Europe, and most of ancient Asia, and did not die out until well into the second century AD when Christianity began its domination of the land. To refresh your memory, the New Testament was written somewhere between 160 and 225 AD, putting it well within the time that Mithraic cults were active. From Mithraic worship come the elements of the Eucharist (though not called that in the cult of Mithra but was called the Lord's Supper), the miter (the headdress that clergy wear), doxology, or hymns to God/the gods, and baptism by water. Mithra was known as the redeemer and he used water to cleanse the sins of man and would feed them bread, water, and wine. Mithra's two animal symbols were the lion and the lamb, and the day of the week associated with Mithraic worship was Sunday, also called Lord's Day. When Mithra died, he was resurrected, like Jesus, and it is interesting to note that the day of his resurrection was celebrated on the spring equinox, or modern Easter. In the book of Revelations 22:16 Jesus says, "I am the root and the offspring of David, and the bright morning star." The traditional Mithraic saying for Mithra, born of the sun was, "I am the star which goes with thee and shines out of the depths."

Moreover, the stars of Orion's belt at certain times of the year will lead one in the direction of the star Sirius, the brightest star in the night sky. Sirius has been a part of many cultures throughout history. This star was of great importance to the ancient Greeks, Romans, Egyptians, and other peoples living in Asia and the Mediterranean; it foretold of summer and crop cycles. It could not be that these three bright stars, sometimes called the Three Kings in days of old, led to the bright star of Sirius, the brightest star in the sky, could it? Sounds like another story we all know.

Jesus Christ—at least that is the name we know Him by now, as that was not His name given at birth. It was simply Jesus, probably Yeshua or some applicable Assyrian name. 'Christ' is a Latin title meaning anointed, and is not a proper name. Jesus Christ was never meant to be the figure and symbol He is known as. It is much more plausible to see how, like Mithra, Jesus was meant to be the next in the line of Solar Messiahs, a God of the Sun, not the Son of God. The messiah concept of Asiatic religions, Mithra worship, was prevalent at that time in history. The sun meant so much to the people, and numerous religions that flourished at the time dealt with sun gods and a few solar messiahs. Mithra was the most notable, and he was the one who had the most impact on the Roman world since the faith was wide-spread and lasted well into the early days of Christianity.

"Life magazine ran an article on the historicity of Jesus, and I was floored to find that they conceded the only evidence we have for his existence is in the Gospels. But don't take Life's word for it. In his book The Quest of the Historical Jesus, the most definitive study that's ever been done on the subject, Albert Schweitzer admitted that there isn't a shred of conclusive proof that Christ ever lived, let alone was the son of God. He concludes that one must therefore accept both on faith."

Another interesting point is the stars themselves and the constellations they form. Some things are proven fact and two of those facts happen to be this: the constellation of Orion is full of big, bright stars. Orion, at certain times of the year, heralds the rising of the star Sirius. Sirius is noted as the brightest star in the night sky, and has been vital to mankind throughout recorded history, so long as man has been watching the stars. Sirius, also called the "dog star", heralds the end of the winter season on planet earth as it rises and stays in orbit during the summer months. Closer to home, our own sun, sol, has a unique relationship with our planet. As we all know, they days in winter grow shorter and shorter because the earth's rotations and orbit puts us further from the sun in winter. As such, the sun's zenith in winter is very low, and the days are short. All of this takes place within the bounds of the Southern Cross, the area of outer space in which all these constellations reside.

These short days culminate in December until a rather odd thing happens. Late into the third week of December, the sun reaches its lowest zenith, barely moving in the sky at all. It stays low in the shortest days of the year, and appears to have no upward movement. This is on December 22nd or so of each year. To an ancient stargazer, it would appear that the sun has died, as it sinks in the sky and for three days does not appear to stir. Three days later, on December 25th, the sun will shift north one degree. It appears to move up, or ascend. From that day the sun will rise higher each day, its zenith increasing, thus heralding longer days and an eventual end to winter. This is not fancy or fiction, but what happens every year, and has since the dawn of our solar system. It is a feat you can note for yourself if you have a telescope, a good eye, and a little patience.

So, we have the sun on the Southern Cross appear to die each year as the earth enters into its winter orbit. Man, of course, did not know that the earth revolved around the sun at this time in history. The sun was ours, and it revolved around us. Psalm 104:5 tells us, "He set the earth on its foundations; it can never be moved." Ancient man, watching the stars, notes that when our sun begins to droop in the sky, descending upon the Southern Cross in which it rests, all one needs do is look for the constellation of Orion and the three bright stars within Orion. Those bright stars will align and to the east will lead them to Sirius. Sirius, in turn, will herald summer as on December 25th our sun's zenith will increase and the days will become longer. Winter will end, crops can grow once again, and the land will support life.

These stellar facts coincide with all solar messiah legends of the time. Mithra, the most notable before the time of Jesus, fell in with His own crowd of solar messiahs. Attis, solar messiah of Phrygia, was also born on December 25th. Attis's mother, Nana, was a virgin, and when Attis died he was resurrected three days later. Adonis, a Hellenistic deity, was a god of annual re-birth of vegetation. What is interesting is that Adonis's mother's name was Myrrha. Jesus, like Attis and Mithra, was born on the 25th of December to a virgin named Mary. The names Mary and Myrrha are significant because of the astrological trait they share. Both names begin with the letter M, both sound almost identical, and both have a counterpart in the stars. The constellation of Virgo, the only female constellation, is also called Virgo the Virgin. She is ruled by the planet Mercury. The sign for Virgo is an altered M, as seen below.

♍

The letter M is not the only key here. Virgo is further symbolized by a maiden who always carries a sheaf of wheat. Virgo represents many things, and the harvest is one of them. She is the wheat bearer, the bread maker, and her home in the stars is aptly named by the ancient Hebrews as Bethlehem. If you translate the word Bethlehem into English from the Hebrew you have house of bread. Thus the Jewish people called the constellation of Virgo the House of Bread and so important was Virgo that a whole city was named for her. To see the evolution from Mithra to Jesus, all one must do is look to the stars, and at the religions that came before. When Constantine and his all male cabinet created the new from the old, they certainly lacked originality. Both Mithra and Jesus share the same birth date, the same birth sequence and story, add some spice by taking a bit from the legend of Attis, and add in the Virgin Virgo where Jesus was born in his House of Bread, or Bethlehem.

Jesus was meant to signify the sun and its light, its power of life and rebirth, and the way it rose each day to chase away the darkness and cause crops to grow. Jesus was meant to be the God-Sun, the immortal one who died each year on the Southern Cross in the night sky. As winter and shorter days approached Sirius would appear, and if you follow the three bright stars of Orion's Belt to find Sirius, the sun would begin its ascent in the sky, heralding longer days and bountiful crops. How blown out of proportion some things can become is simply amazing.
To further the significance of Jesus as a solar messiah rather than the savior of humanity you can take verses from the scriptures themselves.

- John 9:5 "While I am in the world, I am the light of the world."
- John 14: "I will come back and take you to be with me that you also may be where I am. You know the way to the place where I am going."
- Mark 13: "But in those days, following that distress, "the sun will be darkened, and the moon will not give its light; the stars will fall from the sky, and the heavenly bodies will be shaken. At that time men will see the Son of Man coming in clouds with great power and glory." – *Note the word 'son' instead of the intended 'sun'. This is a very telling sign of the way the sun sinks in its zenith in December and of the details above.*

The idea of Jesus is an out and out Xerox of Mithra; most of the similarities are glaringly obvious and not even attempted to be changed overmuch. It did not have to be; people were more or less ignorant of the change from Mithra worship to Jesus worship as they had more pressing matters to tend to at the times. Rome was taxing its people to the point of starvation and riot. The empire was spread thin, and the politicians were lining their pockets while the common folk toiled and suffered.

The obvious difference is the fear factor that Jesus Christ brings with Him. Mithra did not preach slavery, nor did he send non-believers to some lake of fire and eternal torture. That idea is somewhat original to Christianity, and it is the driving force behind the religion's staying power. We will study that, however, at a later point. Suffice it to say that the story of Jesus Christ, when you study it and analyze it to similar religions that flourished before and during this period in history, is just not true. It is not so much lies, but misconstrued stories and unknown science as well as lies.

One must also ask the questions who were the three kings that came to adorn baby Jesus? The bible says only that they are kings, but kings of what cities or provinces? Why did three random kings follow the star of Sirius and come to the city of Bethlehem? Who told them to go? The bible never tells us about these kings, or where they hail from. All we learn from the bible of these kings are their names. That is most likely due to the fact that Jesus is not real, was never "born", and the three kings are but 3 stars in the Orion constellation. Some argue that the bible never calls these three men kings, but wise men, or magi. It is also suggested that these men were priests of some sort. In this case, how did three men from—supposedly—Arabia, Persia, and India know to go and follow the star Sirius? What prompted them to go? Did God tell them to go, or were these men fortune tellers? As we learned earlier, God commands that all witches and fortune tellers **must** be killed, so if that is the case why would God send such people visions? Also, as these three magi were of the East, they would have been either Zoroaster followers or Hindi, possibly even Mithra worshipers.

As we have also learned God commands that we kill priests and people who follow other gods. If that is so, why would God send these three pagan priests to worship and adorn His newborn son? Would not He have the three magi killed on site as they entered the city? This is just more contradiction coming from the bible and more evidence of the complete fabrication of the Jesus myth.

If you look at all early art that depicts Jesus, you will find one of two things, or both: Jesus' head is always enshrined by light, or a circle, and various times with a cross in the back ground. In addition, many images will also show him with the crown of thorns. The ever-present circle represents the halo of light, or the corona of the sun. The cross in the back ground has the dual purpose to represent either the pagan cross of the zodiac to signify the sun's orbit and cycles and/or to represent the Southern Cross of the constellations. The crown of thorns is actually another allegory for sun rays, rays that banish darkness, cause new life and new crops to grow, that sheds light upon the world, and warms all beneath them.

Aside from the bible, which we know was compiled by Emperor Constantine and his cohorts, there are no forms of proof that the figure of Jesus really did exist. Paintings do not count. The bible is a fallible source of information at best and cannot be used as evidence for the simple fact that the book is nothing but untruths, misinterpreted naturally-occurring events, man-made stories, and second and third and fourth-hand accounts of historical events. We know that if Jesus was a real figure that He would have died in or about 33 AD. We also know that the first version of the bible appeared roughly between 40 AD and 225 AD, and many claim it was the year 130 AD. In any case that is a good spread of years, and plenty of time to re-write the Talmud and fabricate the rest.

Do religious people think that Jesus died upon the cross, was resurrected three days later, and when He did that the bible just suddenly appeared? Did it fall from the sky? Did Jesus hand out copies as Hare Krishna's hand out flowers and pamphlets at airports? No, the bible was written a later date, mixed with the stories of the Torah for history and back story, elements of pre-existing and older religions that had the biggest impact on the people and ones that were most readily accepted added in, and the rest based upon what Rome wanted out of its subjects—order and fear.

Aside from the bible there are no true and real documents in regards to a man such as Jesus living at the time. Josephus is the man most cited for creating one of the only works outside of the bible to mention Jesus. His works, however, have always been shown to be convoluted in terms that Josephus was a Jew who opted not to commit suicide like his peers in

Galilee and instead became a Roman citizen. Choosing to keep his head upon his shoulders, Josephus became a Roman apologist at first, and later in life became a Christian apologist, espousing the new tenets of Christianity over his outdated and antiquated Judaism. As such, was Josephus sincere? Was he part of the propaganda machine of the time? His works and words regarding Jesus are not a decent source for proof, as the world will never know if the man wrote those words and accolades of Jesus out of his newly acquired faith or at the point of a Roman sword.

The second source outside of the bible people can cite for "proof" is the writing of Tacitus, a Roman historian and senator. Tacitus was born in 56 AD and died in 117 AD. In his later works he makes a fleeting reference to how and why Emperor Nero burned Rome, and blames the ordeal on Christ and His Christians. Seeing as how Tacitus was not born until after Jesus supposedly lived and died, and the that fledgling religion of Christianity was just taking hold, only means that Tacitus could not have known Jesus as a real person. Tacitus only knew what this new bible was teaching, and what the masses were practicing.

Now, discounting these two fallible sources of information, and knowing we cannot trust the bible, what proof is there? I am to believe that a man-God such as Jesus lived and died, He traveled about with a dozen people and preformed miracles, spread His teachings, and brought upon Himself the wrath of Rome and yet NO ONE chronicled it at the time? Not one sage, not one historian living at the time, not one king or queen of a surrounding province, not one poet, not one scholar, not one Rabbi or polytheist priest.....no one. There are no documents, no books, no scrolls, no writings, and no tablet from the time that Jesus Christ supposedly lived that was written by any person. Every single account, especially the bible, is hearsay and after the fact. If the man was so great, and His teachings so wonderful and miracles were performed, why did no one chronicle them?

Because Jesus never existed outside of metaphor and allegory. Jesus Himself did not leave us one shred of his time on earth if He was real. He was a teacher, a wise man, and a Rabbi. Why did Jesus leave not a single writing of His own? Why did everything He supposedly stood for and teach find its way into the bible and not come from His own hand? Was He illiterate? Was He not actually God Himself? Was He not perfect and omniscient and omnipotent? It makes no sense that such a man, such a being, could not read and write, so why did Jesus leave us nothing?

Again, because Jesus never existed outside of metaphor and allegory. Jesus did not invent a new religion. The figure of Jesus was a Jew, and he preached Judaism with a twist. If what He was teaching was so important why did he not deem to pen (or have penned) a single word of what he was preaching while he was alive? Why did no one else take the initiative to do so if this was such glorious, world-changing stuff? Why was Jesus working in the dark and hiding out from Rome and the Jews if He was the Son of God/God incarnate and bringing light and love to the world? He was hiding out, for Judas supposedly dimed him out for a handful of silver coins. I think you know what I am going to respond with—Jesus never existed, and all accounts of His life were and are fabrications.

Going back to the Torah, every story comes from either second, third, or fourth-hand accounts as well. The stories—and they are just that, stories—are all parables of how to obey, and how events and history may have happened. The Torah, like all religious works, is not meant to be a historical tome. They were not meant to be used as history books. Ultimately that is what they have become, with people believing that what is written in those books is the absolute, word-for-word truth. Those, and all other religion-based texts and books, were meant for control.

Religion is a tool used for controlling, conforming, and quieting. At the time that the Torah was set to writing, most all of the common people were illiterate. Was there some immortal and unerringly attentive scribe that followed people from the time of Adam and Eve up until the book of Revelations ends? If a lone scribe did not put all these verses that seem verbatim on paper, did God have all-night cram sessions with scribes and holy men? Where did all the verses come from? How were they compiled? How do we know that the verses in the scriptures are accurate? Moses supposedly wrote most of the Torah, but Moses was not around during Genesis up to Exodus.

Those of us who have cured ourselves of the disease, or those of us who have never been infected with it, can see it plainly. Men wrote the bible, just as men wrote the Torah. These books were not inspired by any deity, but by men and their greed, their violent ways, with their chauvinism and their loins, and their need to control other men.

Jesus Christ is just another tool that, two centuries after its creation, the elite saw that it fit nicely into the tool box that the Roman Empire was using to dominate its subjects. Hence you have the allegory for the new solar messiah turned into a nightmare God of eternal punishment.

Part II

Let us suppose that Jesus Christ was real, and did indeed walk among us performing miracles. Exactly what miracles did Jesus perform? Reading through the gospels there are accounts of Jesus healing people. Jesus healed a blind man, a deaf man, a bent woman, a mute, cured a boy of fever, restored a missing ear, and healed a few more people of minor maladies. The key word I would like to impress upon is A. Jesus healed A blind man, A bent woman, A boy with fever, A deaf man. If Jesus was so powerful and so benevolent and He was/is God in a human body why not eradicate all maladies? Why not cure blindness, cure diseases like cancer, leprosy, fever, malaria, and plague; heal and restore all amputees, fix all bent people and hunchbacks, and so on. Why cure just a few? Was it beyond the scope of His power? Are we all not worthy of being whole and well? Jesus stilled one storm in his life time. What about the rest? How many storms and earthquakes and tsunamis and cyclones and tornadoes have ravaged the world and have since killed millions?

Jesus also cursed a fig tree. He made it wither away into a husk simply because it was barren of any fruit at the time He happened by. What did a fig tree ever to do to anyone? Figs are wonderful. I happen to love Fig Newtons. Perhaps a farmer had just harvested that tree, or a young boy picked the leaves and fruit for his hungry family? Perhaps there was a drought (an act of God?) and the tree had not the fortitude to bear fruit.

Jesus supposedly preformed exorcisms, removing demons from the bodies of humans. One time he "allowed" a horde of demons he had just exorcised to possess a herd of swine. Once the herd was possessed, the pigs dashed themselves off the cliffs and into the sea where they all drowned. Jesus is quite lucky PETA was not there; else He would have some angry people to deal with.

Jesus walked on water, and turned water into wine. He also fed thousands of people on two separate occasions with just a few loaves of bread and a few fish. As above with disease and sickness, why not end starvation? It certainly seems within His power, yet it is not done. We must also note that every miracle supposedly preformed is a miracle that leaves behind no evidence, not a single shred or proof. You would think a man-God would do something like etch his face in a mountainside, or create a floating city, or do something profound and ever-lasting.

Instead he curses a fig tree, calms a single storm, makes some pigs suicidal, and cures a few sick people. Is that it? What a monumental waste of omnipotence. What a grand waste of cosmic power. The powers of all creation at His fingertips and He gets angry at a tree. It is almost comical that a perfect being gets mad at a fig tree. That people flock to this figure and cannot see the forest through the [fig] trees really does amaze me.

Not only is Jesus all-too stingy with His supposed miracles, but He lies as well. Yes, that's right, Jesus lied, and numerous times. I count eight times that Jesus made bold-faced lies, all in His own words. Well, you must take that with a grain of salt; the quotes come from the books of the apostles. Jesus makes promises He cannot keep, and also lies about the power of prayer. Since I have made such a bold statement, I will reproduce the quotes from the scriptures.

- John 15:7 "If you remain in me and my words remain in you, ask whatever you wish, and it will be given you."
- John 14:12 "I tell you the truth, anyone who has faith in me will do what I have been doing. He will do even greater things than these, because I am going to the Father. And I will do whatever you ask in my name, so that the Son may bring glory to the Father. You may ask me for anything in my name, and I will do it."
- John 16:23 "In that day you will no longer ask me anything. I tell you the truth, my Father will give you whatever you ask in my name. Until now you have not asked for anything in my name. Ask and you will receive, and your joy will be complete."
- John 15:16 "You did not choose me, but I chose you and appointed you to go and bear fruit—fruit that will last. Then the Father will give you whatever you ask in my name."
- Matthew 21:21 "Jesus replied, "I tell you the truth, if you have faith and do not doubt, not only can you do what was done to the fig tree, but also you can say to this mountain, 'Go, throw yourself into the sea,' and it will be done. If you believe, you will receive whatever you ask for in prayer."
- Matthew 18:19 "Again, I tell you that if two of you on earth agree about anything you ask for, it will be done for you by my Father in heaven. For where two or three come together in my name, there am I with them."
- Matthew 7:7 "Ask and it will be given to you; seek and you will find; knock and the door will be opened to you. For everyone who asks receives; he who seeks finds; and to him who knocks, the door will be opened."
- Luke 11:9 "So I say to you: Ask and it will be given to you; seek and you will find; knock and the door will be opened to you. For everyone who asks receives; he who seeks finds; and to him who knocks, the door will be opened. Which of you fathers, if your son asks for a fish, will give him a snake instead? Or if he asks for an egg, will give him a scorpion? If you then, though you are evil, know how to give good gifts to your children, how much more will your Father in heaven give the Holy Spirit to those who ask Him!"

In all of the above quotes from Jesus, we see that He says whatever you pray for, whatever you ask of Him or God for, it shall be done. I will assume that only the faithful get this benefit, but even then Jesus is making promises He cannot keep, and showing us that prayer, even by the faithful, goes unheeded and unanswered. In my eyes, if a faithful person acts according to the verses above, the wish or prayer should be answered immediately—not in week, or a year, or in ten years, or at some future point, but at the moment. The wish should also be answered in a direct, as-asked-for way, not in some fashion, or some near and cryptic way. Working in mysterious ways, and good things comes to those who wait are B.S. answers to my argument. If what Jesus and God say is to be held as the truth, then a prayer should be answered straight away. We all know this is not the case, for the world would be a different place.

If you wish to make excuses and delude yourself on this, please feel free. The fact that you **must** do so only proves the point, and makes any opposing argument moot, and shows that that prayer, Jesus, and ultimately God, is not real.

> *"Jehovah was not a moral god. He had all the vices and he lacked all the virtues. He generally carried out all his threats, but he never faithfully kept a promise."*
> Robert Green Ingersoll, 1833 – 1899

Part III: Jesus vs. Joseph

It is a fact that the figure of Joseph from the Torah shares more than twenty similarities with Jesus Christ. These similarities are not simply common traits; the two share more than just names beginning with the letter J. From the miracle of their birth, to the number of brothers/disciples, to their time in Egypt, to the age they started their respective ministries, to death and beyond, the two are the same. If, after all is said and done, one cannot see that Jesus Christ is but a reincarnation of not only Mithra, but of the Hebrew figure of Joseph as well, than one truly has "blind" faith.

The tale of the Tape

Joseph	Vs.	Jesus
Born to a wealthy, powerful father, Genesis 37:3		The Son of God, Matthew 3:17
Taken to Egypt to avoid death, Genesis 37:2		Taken to Egypt to avoid death, John 10:11
Was a Sheppard, Genesis 37:28		Was a Sheppard, Matthew 2:13
Began his ministry at age 30, Genesis 41:46		Began his ministry at age 30, Luke 3:23
Humble and not wealthy, Genesis 45:7		Humble and not wealthy, John 13:12
Instructed by God, Genesis 45:16		Instructed by God, John 5:19
Expressed love & tolerance, Genesis 45:15		Expressed love & tolerance, John 13:14
Gave bread to the hungry, Genesis 41:57		Gave bread to the hungry, Mark 6:41
Had visions of the future, Genesis 37:6		Had visions of the future, Matthew 24:3
Sold for the price of a slave, Genesis 37:28		Sold for the price of a slave, Matthew 26:15
Persecuted for his teachings, Genesis 37:8		Persecuted for his teachings, John 7:7
Falsely accused, Genesis 39:14		Falsely accused, Mark 14:56
Silent at trial, Genesis 39:20		Silent at trial, Mark 15:4

There are many other similarities; most notably that Joseph had twelve brothers and Jesus had twelve disciples. Are all these just coincidences? I think not. Above all, the figure of Jesus is a copy of not only Mithra, but of Joseph. Most shocking is the recent discovery of a tablet in Jordan, near the Dead Sea.

The tablet that was discovered and brought to light in July of 2008 seals the fate of any originality that Christendom can claim. A nearly three-foot long tablet with eighty-seven engraved and inked lines in ancient Hebrew describes the birth of a messiah, a savior to be born and arise from the dead after three days. This tablet dates back to mere decades before the time of Christ. When this tablet is combined with the already prevailing dogma of Mithra—and of the Talmudic Joseph—we see how easy it is for a new religion to come to life. We see how easy the transition from Mithra to Jesus is, now that even the Jews themselves have laid the groundwork for the creation of a new messiah. All the Romans had to do was to capitalize on the superstitious and always-fearful Jews and their monotheistic, chauvinistic, fear-driven religion. It seems the original sin of the universe is not greed, or pride, or gluttony, but man's own gullibility and lack of better judgment.

"I never cease being dumbfounded by the unbelievable things people believe."
Leo Rosten, 1908 – 1997

"If everyone is thinking alike, then someone isn't thinking."
General George S. Patton, 1885 – 1945

Seven: Something old, something new, something borrowed, something blue.

No, this chapter is not about weddings or marriage. As we have seen, Christianity can claim almost nothing that is original. Its tenets, its back story, its elements, and its mythology are all from other religions and cultures. There is one thing that is unique, but that is for later a chapter—I like to keep you in suspense. The one thing Christianity is good at is plagiarism. It plagiarized Roman paganism, Persian paganism, Egyptian paganism, and also Judaism. They say that plagiarism is the sincerest form of flattery, but Christians cannot claim all the glory here. The Jews plagiarized much to come up with their own tyrannical religion, and its folk heroes. Now that we have established that the bible is not a valid source we can turn to for truth, let us see how this, and other religions, have plagiarized and taken from each other.

We know that Judaism most likely had its roots in Egyptian and Persian monotheism. We do not need to revisit that information, but we can look into one of Judaism's greatest assets. Moses. Moses is the greatest hero of the Old Testament, the man who made the Pharaoh release the Jewish people from the bonds of slavery, and then led them to a greater glory. We can debunk that in a coming chapter, but for now let's start by demystify the man himself.

Like Jesus, Moses was an allegorical figure. It is more than likely that the man did not ever exist. Like Jesus, Moses left no [other] writings whatsoever. He supposedly wrote the first five books of the Torah, called the Peneteuch, but an odd discrepancy lies within. Moses is said to have died at the age of 122 years old; still strong in mind and body he just keeled over and died. He was buried anonymously in an unmarked grave where, to this day, no one can find him. Those are the words, more or less, from Deuteronomy 34. It seems awfully convenient that one of the greatest human figures in history gets such secretive burial. The Pharaohs had temples and pyramids created for them upon death. You would think a man who spoke to God and did His work would get a better burial. Moses dies in Deuteronomy, the fifth book of the Peneteuch, so who fully wrote it? Who, then, finished it? It is a contradiction and exposes that Moses did not write the [full] Peneteuch, and was likely not a real person.

Everything about Moses' deeds and actions is all third-person, or more. "Moses said" or "Moses did" is not proof. Moses shares another trait with Jesus, and that is his entire back story is a copy. Just as the story of Jesus was hobbled together mostly from the story of Joseph and Mithra, so, too, was Moses created to fill a much-need gap. I told you the stories of Mithra, Dionysus, Attis, Horus, and Joseph. Are you ready for another story?

Let us meet Sargon of Akkad. Akkad was an empire of Sumerian and Semitic people that flourished around 22 to 24 BC, and was located in Persia, or modern-day Iraq. Although Sargon was a warrior-king, and he is famous for having established a multi-ethnic empire that was both wide-spread and short-lived, Sargon was a real person. He is a legitimate Persian king with a rather interesting life story.

Sargon, you see, was born illegitimately to a ranking priestess, one who was not the king's wife. Sargon's father, presumably a king of the lands of Azupiranu (a Persian land near the Euphrates River), would have had the baby killed to avoid shame, so Sargon's mother placed her baby in basket of reeds and set him adrift upon the Euphrates. He was found by a kindly woman who held some rank in the city and Sargon gained favor as he grew. From humble beginnings as a gardener Sargon attained kingship over the province, having been blessed by his god, Ishtar. That part is debatable, but Sargon did rule a nation, and his ways lasted over one hundred and fifty years.

Hmmm….a mother placed a baby in a reed basket, set him adrift upon the river so he would not be killed, raised by an influential woman and attained notoriety with the city. Does this sound familiar? The fact that the story of Sargon of Akkad predates both the story of Moses and the Jewish religion is a pretty good sign that Sargon's story was blatantly plagiarized by the Jews. Since Sargon's empire—and please remember it was a multi-ethnic empire, sure to have Egyptians, Phoenicians, and especially Hyksos—flourished and its influence was evident in the Nile delta, it would have been easy for any and all civilizations to hear of and assimilate its ways and cultures.

Despite the monumental similarities between Sargon and Moses, we must add one more man to this equation. Please meet Karna of the Hindi religion: he was born of the Sun God and a human woman via an immaculate conception. Upon his birth the mother, not wanting to face the world as an unwed mother, placed Karna in a box and set him adrift on the river whereupon he was found by a king and his wife and raised as such. There are many such stories about illegitimate children, or ones that are "prophesized" to end a king's rule and henceforth told to be put to death, only to be spared. Gilgamseh, Perseus, Romulus, Moses, Karna, Sargon, Oedipus, and so many others share this back story, and almost all of them predate Judaism. Whether they are real men or men of legends and folk tales, the stories of Sargon and Moses are an age-old narrative and a model for those that have come after. Moses, most likely, never existed. The people that fled Egypt, for whatever reason took with them bits and pieces of all sorts of religious and cultural ways. Is it so hard to reason that they, when they made their own culture and religion, plagiarized?

The two most relevant and striking plagiarisms perpetrated by Judaism are enough, on their own, to discredit the entire structure of the religion. The first major plagiarism comes from one of the world's oldest recorded creations myths. The Sumerians, a people whose society and religious tenets and beliefs date back much further than the Jewish people, believed creation came about by the great pantheon of gods. Their gods lived in generations, and it took six generations of gods to create the heavens and the earth. The sixth generation, finally growing smart, used their energy to create mankind so that man could continue the gods' work, but more importantly so that the seventh generations of gods could rest. The gods used their own, red blood mixing it with the earth to create man. The Sumerian word for such red dirt is called *adamah*, and the name Adam is a derivative of that word.

Six generations of gods to create the heavens and earth, six days for God to create the heavens and earth. The seventh generation of gods could rest, on the seventh day God rested. The gods created mankind with *adamah*, God created man out of dirt and named him Adam…

Also from the Sumerian mythos comes the tale of Eniki. This male god set foot in an area of time and space that belonged to his fellow goddess Ninhurgag. This area, Ninhurgag's garden, was sacred to Her, and Eniki snuck in and ate fruits from her trees. Eniki's trespass and taking of her sacred fruits angered Her, so She caused her fellow immortal to fall to earth, and the fall gave the god seven wounds. Later, Ninhurgag decided to forgive Eniki, and came and bore him seven daughters, one for each wound. The daughters were also restorative, and each daughter conceived cured one of the wounds. Ninti, the daughter of Eniki's ribs, closed the wounds in His chest.

Eniki trespassed in a scared garden and ate fruit he knew he was not supposed to. Eve ate fruit from a tree she from which she was bade not to. Ninti, a female, was born from Eniki's ribs. Eve, a female, was made from Adam's rib. It is key to note, however, that the Sumerian people were more tolerant of women, and that the people who became the Jews were much less so; Eniki was a male god who was punished by a female goddess, and a female goddess was the one who forgave her peer and healed his wounds. Males in the primitive culture that became Judaism would never stand for such actions, as women were severely inferior to them, and were treated as property, to be subservient to man.

But now you do see that the two basic and grandly important myths that are the start of Judaism, and ultimately Christianity, are nothing but recycled Sumerian stories. There are no ifs, ands, or buts about the validity of the Sumerian myths, and there is no argument with which to counter that the ancient Jewish people did nothing but plagiarize their Sumerian predecessors.

Such actions are so common in the ancient world. Religions and beliefs prospered from the start of human society up through the last century, fueled by open and blind acceptance in tandem with wildly superstitious people, little to no scientific understanding, the lack of literacy, and the control religious institutions held over the common folk. Now, with our amazing scientific discoveries and our greater understanding of the world and the universe around us, religion still thrives. It does so because even after all our thousands of years of evolving as a species, mankind has yet to outgrow his basic fears and superstitions. It is belittling to our race that we now know so much, yet fail to let go of outdated, archaic, sadistic, and repressive ideas and notions that serve us no good.

Part II

"You can find things in the traditional religions which are very benign and decent and wonderful and so on, but I mean, the Bible is probably the most genocidal book in the literary canon. The God of the Bible - not only did He order His chosen people to carry out literal genocide - I mean, wipe out every Amalekite to the last man, woman, child, and, you know, donkey and so on, because hundreds of years ago they got in your way when you were trying to cross the desert - not only did He do things like that, but, after all, the God of the Bible was ready to destroy every living creature on earth because some humans irritated Him. That's the story of Noah. I mean, that's beyond genocide - you don't know how to describe this creature. Somebody offended Him, and He was going to destroy every living being on earth? And then He was talked into allowing two of each species to stay alive - that's supposed to be gentle and wonderful."
Noam Chomsky, 1928 –

Flood. When one hears the word it instantly conjures an ancient image, does it not? I cannot speak for the rest of humankind, but when I hear the word 'flood' I immediately think of Noah, his ark, and the whole story, and I am an anti-theist! That story has been ingrained into most all of humans. I bring up the word 'flood' now because we are on the topic of plagiarism. The biblical story of the flood, of Noah, the ark, and all that comes with it is nothing original, at least not as far as the Torah is concerned. It is evident that I like telling stories, so here is yet another one.

The Epic of Gilgamesh. I read this book in eighth grade; I went to a college prep school, and my eighth grade English and History teacher, Mr. Aiello—he was a great teacher, I do recall—was big into ancient history. We studied mythology, the Greeks, the Romans, The Norse, the Egyptians, and more. We read books like the colossal *Peloponnesian War,* and shorter *The Epic of Gilgamesh.* If you read the story of Gilgamesh, who was another very real person, you will find a few things that are quite interesting.

A Mesopotamian king, fifth king of the nation of Uruk during the twenty-third and twenty-second centuries BC, Gilgamesh claimed his mother was a goddess and his father was human. He created an empire with his superhuman deeds as told in the Epic of Gilgamesh. The work itself is one of the earliest known books, and is quite possibly the world's first and oldest novel. One of Gilgamesh's great deeds was to erect a huge wall to protect his people and his empire, a wall that, centuries later, Sargon of Akkad claims he brought down with his own might.

These are not the interesting things, however. What is interesting is that, according to the Epic of Gilgamesh, Gilgamesh sets off upon a quest to meet a man named Utnapishtim, an immortal, as Gilgamesh claims to be. Utnapishtim tells the story of how, long ago, the Mesopotamian gods were going to make a flood to kill all of mankind, as humans were not what the gods thought they were cracked up to be. The god Ea, the god who had created humans, did not want this, and so He Himself went to Utnapishtim to warn him. Ea told Utnapishtim to craft a huge boat, giving dimensions and how to seal it with pitch, take upon it all sorts of animals, and save mankind. Ea also tells Utnapishtim how to test for dry land by releasing birds. In the epic we learn that Utnapishtim's ark hits dry land in the reaches of Mount Nisir, which is only a few hundred miles away from the infamous Mount Ararat.

This popular Mesopotamian story, widely known throughout the Nile delta, predates the Judaic story of Noah by many, many centuries. The only real difference is that the biblical flood lasted forty days and nights and the flood as related to Gilgamesh lasted just under a week. In the paragraph above, the keywords are "long ago." If this tale of flood and mayhem occurred long ago, then how long ago? Where there is smoke there is fire, and I do have a theory on that. It is borrowed from science and perhaps other men incalculably more intelligent than I, but you will have to wait for the next chapter to hear it.

Again, we can see how the early Jews did nothing but assimilate the tales of Gilgamesh and weave them, rather un-originally, with other stories to fashion a religion; flattering to the tales and legends and religions of days past, but unimpressive to anyone who studies history and ancient cultures.

> *"I find the whole business of religion profoundly interesting. But it does mystify me that otherwise intelligent people take it seriously."*
> Douglass Adams, 1952 – 2001

Lastly, there are two other possible ways that natural events could shape the stories of man. We know that early man was a superstitious creature, and anything that happened in nature that humans could not easily comprehend was written-off as an act of the gods. If we travel back in time to roughly 1,500 to 1,700 BC and take a vacation in the Greek Isles, we will find ourselves in a precarious predicament; the volcano of the island of Santorini erupted around that time, and it was a pyroclasm of great magnitude. The blast not only filled the air with many cubic tons of ash and debris, but caused tidal waves that reached as far as Africa. Such eruptions are common throughout history, but early man would record such events within their myths and legends, and pass the stories down through the generations. It is well within limits to assume that people entwined such floods, such times of darkness (due to airborne ash clouds), and other natural phenomena into religion. We certainly see it with the story of Noah and his Sumerian predecessor.

Another very likely culprit of a flood story would have us travel back even farther in history to 10,000 to 13,000 BC. We know that the last great ice age took place at that point in time, and it covered most of North America (all the way from Canada to approximately Ohio), much of Northern Europe, and there were many glaciers and ice sheets in middle Asia, just above India and close to what was then Persia. If the summers during the ice age were cool the ice would have melted very slowly, and the melt waters would meander to the sea. When the ice age finally gave way and if summers began to become their usual, brutal selves, the ice sheets and glaciers would have melted rapidly. I would not want to be around when that happened, even with a good wetsuit, a life vest, and a surfboard.

The flood produced by massive glaciers and ice sheets melting would be profound. Rivers, for years after the melt, would be high and turbulent. Early man would be impacted greatly, and the story of the flood would worm its way down from generation-to-generation. If you look back through history, and look at what modern science can help us learn about the history of our world, it is not very hard to see the tinder and sparks that ignited so much myth and religion.

"Religion is another matter. Religion -- or at least Christianity -- insists that certain things be considered facts, based purely on faith. In other words, you are supposed to believe, just because the religious view says to. The faithful will tell you, for example, that God exists in fact, in spite of the total lack of empirical evidence for God's existence. If pressed for evidence, they will come up with a series of irrational statements like, "Well, the world couldn't possibly exist unless God made it," or "There has to be a reason for all this to exist." According to the religious world-view, too, all of creation exists for the benefit of man."
Morris Sullivan, 1956 -

Part III

Judeo-Christianity is also the parent of two other religions: Mormonism and Islam. Islam, being much older than Mormonism, traces its roots back to the early 600's AD, and has aspects of both religions. Mormonism is a direct descendent of Christianity, and is a relatively new faith (circa the mid 1800's AD). As with every religion, both claim to be the only true religion of the world, and its practitioners vehemently believe so.

Mormonism is a faith that has some auspicious origins. According to Mormon history, the story begins in the 1800's in America. A young man, Joseph Smith Jr., who is concerned about his own Christian faith, kneels in his up-state New York home to pray. He is met by an angel sent by God and the angel tells young Mr. Smith to go to a certain spot in the woods, and a tree will be pointed out. When he gets there, the angel reveals some mysterious tablets made of gold as well as two special "seer stones" with which to translate the tablets. After about a decade this farm boy reveals his works as the first Book of Mormon. Finally decoded, the original tablets magically teleport back to heaven.

The tablets tell a story of how Jewish people living in the Assyrian lands left the deserts on ships they built, and sailed to the New World of America. Once there they built mighty cities and raised huge armies, fighting massive wars, and moved away from the true faith of God. As such they became savages and their cities and armies fell, and not until the golden tablets were to be found and decoded would the glory of God be upon them once again. Moreover, the resurrected Jesus Christ, after his resurrection and before ascending into heaven, came to the Americas and preached the gospel.

Ask any non-Mormon and they will tell you that the story is insane. Well it is, but that is beside the point. Why is that story insane? We all know that Jews did not build boats and sail the seas to occupy America. There are no archeological finds of massive cities left by these people, no fields of bones, armor, or weapons left by these huge wars. There are no graves, no artifacts, and no writings left by said people. There are no marks of these societies left by these people on the native Americans be it in their culture, their traditions, their language, their weaponry, their writings and stories. Nothing! The idea itself is pure fancy, but a Mormon believes this as the absolute truth. They can come up with a thousand explanations and excuses why there is no evidence to this fairy tale, but none that satisfy basic logic, science, or history.

Moreover, Joseph Smith Jr. initially supported slavery and the slave owners in the States. The Mormon movement as a whole banned blacks from attaining priesthood, or being an ordained Mormon minister, and it was not until June of 1978 that this ban was removed—further evidence of how religion separates by what we humans call 'race.'

I like to believe that we are all one race. Black and Latino are not races. Asian and European, white and Brazilian are not races. Feline is a race. Canine and bovine are races. Insects and arachnids are races. Fish and crustaceans are all races. Asian, Latino, black, white, ect…are ethnic descriptions they are breeds. They are demographics, not races. Human, *homo-sapiens,* is the race, but I digress.

Now we come to Jews and Christians; tell them that the story of Mormonism is true and they will scoff at you, laugh at you, and call the premises and ideas of this religion preposterous. Ask them about the old Norse legends that say the remains of an Ice Giant (Ymir) killed by Odin is what he fashioned the Earth with, or tell them about ancient Babylonian creeds that teach Marduk killed a dragon named Tiamat and used her body to fashion the earth and the sky and you are off your rocker. Plumed dragon-gods, like Quetzalcoatl of the Aztecs, are not real and huge men with one eye like the Cyclopes, or Jews that built ships with which to navigate oceans to build vast civilizations on American soil are obviously a farce ….but a virgin woman can give birth to the son of a god? A man can part an ocean with a stick of wood? A man can die and be resurrected? A bush can burn for all time yet never burn out? A star can leave its orbit and show three men how to find a city? A man can walk on water and feed five thousand people with two fish and some bread? If you behave and fear appropriately you can either live forever or suffer eternal torment for not believing accordingly? It is a case of the pot calling the kettle black. The bubble of delusion Jews and Christians live in is the same that all people of one faith or another live within: only their religion is the right one, and all others are false.

What should also be noted that all three religions, Judaism, Christianity, and Mormonism preach that infidels should be killed. All three religions supposedly represent the same God, yet in all of them we have tenets to kill non-believers. There are more verses from each respective book than is below about death and torment for non-believers, but here a few of them.

- In the following books and verses of the bible you will find commands from God to <u>kill</u> non-believers, people that follow other gods, blasphemers, people of a different religion, and "infidels". 2 Chronicles 15:12, Exodus 22:19,

Deuteronomy 13:7 & 13:13, Deuteronomy 17:2, Leviticus 24:10, and Romans 1:24.

- In the Book of Mormon, in 1 Nephi 22:14 "And every nation which shall war against thee, O house of Israel, shall be turned one against another, and they shall fall into the pit which they digged to ensnare the people of the Lord. And all that fight against Zion shall be destroyed, and that great whore, who hath perverted the right ways of the Lord, yea, that great abominable church, shall tumble to the dust and great shall be the fall of it." In Nephi 4:13 it teaches "It's better to kill one person than have a whole nation die unbelievers." The Book of Alma is full of atrocities committed against Native American Indians for the sole reason of their darker skin and "heathen" ways. In Alma 8:16 and 9:12 God says He will kill all people who will not repent. Alma 1 teaches Mormons that all who do not belong to the Church of Mormon are lazy, wicked, idolatrous, babbling, murdering thieves.

Eight: Killing Two Myths with One Stone

Science is an amazing thing. It is the greatest tool we humans have in our arsenal. Science is also a matter-of-fact entity. Science does not care about popularity, belief, or morals. It just is. Scientific laws could care less if anyone believes in them or not. Gravity does not care if people do not accept it. Physics and quantum physics do not care if people accept their ways and means or not. Evolution is not bothered by the fact that people choose not to believe it happened (and is still happening). Plugging your ears and singing loudly, or putting on rose-colored glasses is all well and good, but does not change the fact that certain laws and truths of the universe exist. People cling to faith-based doctrine instead of science out of fear and ego.

I am not a scientist, though at one time in my life I did want to be a paleontologist. I am still fascinated by dinosaurs and other extinct animals. No, I do not believe in the Loch Ness Monster, Bigfoot, or other such crypto-zoological beasties. I also look at the little, every-day things and see wonder in them. I do not need religion or fairytales to amaze me; I can pick up a rock and be in awe. How old is this rock that I hold? As old as we know the earth is, at 4.5 billion years old? Is this rock older, as we also know that the planet on which we live was created some 9.5 billion years after whatever forces created the big bang? Could this rock have come from a comet or asteroid that is much older than our planet?

Do not get jumpy that I said "created" or "whatever forces". Just because I/we do not know something does not mean we need to add a God of the Gaps, and I am not doing so. Like I had said, I am not a scientist, but do have basic knowledge of things like Planck Time and the theory of conservation of mass/energy, and other such scientific ideas. There are cosmic forces that are not gods at work, and we do not understand them yet. Yet. As for "created", our planet was created, but not in a few days or by the will of a god. It was created by cosmic trash floating around the universe; rocks, ice, metals, comets, asteroids, and debris cast off and out by the big bang coalesced into orbs as the gravitational pulls of stars/suns caught them and locked them into orbits. There is so much wonder to be found in nature and science that all religions pale beside these discoveries.

I have told a few stories, even a joke, and now I'd like to interject an anecdote of mine. You're either loving me or cursing me by now, so let's feed what you are feeling a little more with this one.

A few years back a local Chasidic Rabbi came to my place of business. The owner of where I work donates to a few select charities and does some advertising with local religious establishments. Anyway, the Rabbi, while here, comes into to speak with me, say hello, kibitz a little. I was born and raised [very reformed] Jewish. I only became the anti-theist I am now shortly before my Bar Mitzvah at age 13, so for me to speak with a Rabbi is not big deal. While there, the Rabbi comes into my office, and notices a little thing I have on my wall. It was left here by the previous person who had occupied this office, and I liked it, so I kept it. It is a fist-sized rock that has been smoothed down and worn by time, and atop of it is an image of the Egyptian goddess Isis, Goddess of Magic and the Nile. It's pretty, so I kept it all these years.

The Rabbi and I get to talking, and he noticed the rock on my wall and asked if I had been to Egypt or Israel, and I told him "no". I honestly forget how the conversation started, but I stated my wonder at the rock on which the image was carved. I recall saying that the image was fairly new—probably done in Cairo to sell to tourists—but the rock itself could be billions of years old. The Rabbi looked at me and deadpanned, "But Michael, don't you know that the earth is only 6,000 years old?"

That was all the prodding I needed to get into a discussion. As it goes, the Rabbi said some things to me that I will not only never forget, but also let me know that to hold a rational, sensible dialogue/debate with someone who is religious is not possible. On the subject of age, and speaking of dinosaurs and such, the Rabbi prompted me to explain how we know that the rock is over 6,000 years old, since the bible says otherwise. Simple, I had said, as we can carbon date the rock, the rocks of the world, the dinosaur and other animal bones we unearth, to see how old they are through radio-carbon dating. We have electron microscopes and other amazing instruments that define age. The reply I got floored me.

He told me in a patronizing way, as if I were some dumb knave, that "God flaws all such machines we make. Every time man invents a machine God will not allow it, and puts flaws into it. It is not our right to question or test God, but to have faith. The bones were put there by God for us to find and explore and test us, not for us to test or question Him." I was silent for a few seconds, my face screwed up in pensive query, and I retorted with a very out of character, "I think that is the most stupid thing I have ever been told, and only a shmuck would say such things. I cannot talk to you anymore." With that I invited him to leave my office. My reply was pretty much verbatim, and I did paraphrase the Rabbi a bit. Truth sure is stranger than fiction, not that an orthodox person of any religion would recognize the truth even if it slapped them in the face.

The religious people would have the rest of the world believe that proof is irrelevant, or somehow a flaw or test set forth by God must be involved. They have to make more excuses on God's behalf rather than accept that their religion is the thing that is flawed. Denial does not justify faith; you can deny dinosaurs all you like, you can argue that they lived alongside Adam and Eve but were all killed in Noah's flood (as ludicrous and immeasurably ignorant as that is), but the fact is that these 'terrible lizards' once held dominion over this blue-covered rock. God flaws machines….what an asinine statement. Is God so insecure that He feels the need to put flaws into machinery created by lesser beings? The only answer would be derogatory and would not favor God, and so I will leave it to your imagination.

Back to this book, however, I would like to use history and science to debunk two more myths that the bible would have us believe: The exodus out of Egypt and the twelve plagues. Thanks to what we are able to know via our technology and through a combination of science and history, these two events can be exposed for exactly what they are, and, more importantly, what they are not. The firestorm of this revelation of how we now know what really happened in the Nile delta so many eons ago is a big one. Just like with dinosaur bones, earth strata, ice core samples, and radio-carbon dating, we know the earth is not 6,000 years old, but 4 plus billion years old. We also now know that a large volcano on Santorini Island erupted around 1,500 to 1,650 BC, and that the event was cataclysmic. You can totally, scientifically, and factually decode, explain, and de-mystify the exodus from Egypt and the twelve plagues with one stone; Santorini.

Part I: The Plagues

Fact is indeed stranger than fiction. It is a fact that the volcano on Santorini erupted as far back as 1,500 BC. For the laymen reading this, Santorini is an Island near Greece, and not too far from the African and western-most parts of the Middle East. This one natural disaster triggered a chain of events that took years to come to fruition, but when they did, it was like nothing man at the time had encountered before. The un-scientific and deathly superstitious men at this time dealt with these events as only they knew how; it was the wrath of some god. Thankfully today we know better.

When Santorini erupted, it blasted more than seven cubic miles of magma and ash over twenty miles in the air. The resulting backlash from such an explosion caused earth tremors and tidal waves that reached as far as the coast of Africa. Aside from the darkness the ash cloud would produce, the effects of such a sudden and tumultuous change to the earth's atmosphere would cause hail and lightning at the same time. Furthermore, what goes up must come down. Lava ejected more than twenty miles in the air has to come back down, and as it did some invariably turned into hail, and some stayed as globules of lava. This takes care of three of the plagues right there: darkness, fire, and hail. The ash cloud would also change the weather patterns for some time to come, and cause an increase in sandstorms.

The plague of drought is easily explained by the huge ash cloud from the eruption and the resulting increase in sandstorms. Such a cloud of ash would reduce humidity via a reverse greenhouse effect, and rain would not fall.

Drought and heat will readily dry up smaller ponds and rivers. Any acid rain could easily turn the Nile River red with pollution. Sudden floods due to the tidal waves the eruption produced could dislodge huge amounts of the red clay and red sediment prevalent in the Nile to turn the river red, but it is more feasible that the amazing amount of carbon gas build up beneath the tectonic plates of the European and African continents turned the Nile red. The gasses that seeped up through the cracks in the tectonic plates can and will—and still do—turn the Nile crimson. Another plague down.

The unhealthy environment in the Nile River would cause many of the other plagues to occur. Fish would die in staggering amounts as oxygen is removed from the water. The frogs living in the now polluted river would escape to the land in mass numbers, and what animals feed on lice and flies? Fish and Frogs. No fish and frogs mean that lice, flies, mosquitoes, and gnats could all experience a population explosion. As we all know, lice, flies, and mosquitoes transmit disease. A population explosion of said insects would infect man and beast alike, and boils, malaria, sickness, cattle disease, fever blisters, and skin defects would occur in record numbers. With no fresh rain and a river red with what the ancients thought was blood, I am pretty sure not a lot of bathing took place, and the filth only caused the diseases to breed and spread. Bang! Bang! More plagues shot down with the smoking gun of reason and science. Locusts are next.

We know that locusts have a seventeen-year cycle. They come out in mass (swarms can number in the billions), eat all plant-based life around, and then mate and lay eggs after which they die. If the locusts' cycle was taking place somewhere around the time of this entire calamity caused by the Santorini eruption, the hectic weather in the delta would explain why the locusts would descend upon a desert city. Supposed a swarm of millions or billions of locusts try to make their way across the desert, but frequent sand storms, or even the original ash cloud itself, forces them down to land? Locusts explained.

Lastly we have Gabriel, the Angel of Death (funny, you'd think that would be an oxymoron, but no one calls it that way). Death of the first born. The twelfth plague. Explain that, will you? You cannot, and so it must be God! I can explain it, and I have one word for you: Cameroon.

Cameroon is a province of West Africa, and Nykos village is in Cameroon, near Lake Nykos. During the night of August 21, 1986, the angel of death paid Africa another visit. This time it did not see any doorways painted with lamb's blood, so it killed almost the entire village of Nykos; 1,746 people to be exact, plus thousands of cattle, dogs, goats, sheep, and other animals. Was it Gabrielle again? No, it was carbon dioxide gas.

The massive amounts of carbon dioxide gas under the lake and within the lake itself succumbed to natural pressures and exploded from the lake. A resulting cloud of deadly gas over 100 million cubic meters wide covered the valley of Lake Nykos. As carbon gas is heavier than air, it sunk to the ground, and the immense toxicity of the cloud killed people and animals instantly and silently for twelve miles around. This same scenario also played out in 1984 when thirty-seven were similarly killed in the village near Lake Monoun, also in Cameroon.

Carbon dioxide gas is deadly to non-plant life, but not in small clouds and not when it is carried away by air currents. It could kill a single small animal if it was hanging out or sleeping by an earth-bound gas vent, but otherwise the gas is harmless due to the fact that it is released slowly, and carried away by wind to be absorbed by water and by plants.

This sort of gas leak is common on the African continent, so why could it not happen in Egypt? It is much more likely, much more believable that a severe and deadly carbon dioxide leak overtook certain parts of Egypt rather than a vengeful god sending an angel to earth to kill first-born sons. Occam's Razor, my friend, or as we like to paraphrase, "All other things being equal, the simplest solution is the best."

We do not know in which order these "plagues" took place, but we can assemble them by their nature. These plagues could have happened within a single generation, or have taken longer, and all or any of them could force an exodus of people out of Egypt. Perhaps even the timeline is off by a few hundred years, and the eruption of Santorini had taken place during the Armana Era of Egypt during Amonhotep IV's rule. The era was certainly ripe with disease, plague, and maladies. Perhaps they combined and forced an exodus. Perhaps, when the Armana Era ended, the "plague" era began, and those combined elements forced an exodus.
Any of these elements could spell disaster in many ways for people, most notably horrendous living conditions and/or horrendous business conditions. In any case and for whatever reason, we know that some sort of exodus took place, and that many Hyksos and other pre-Semitic people left Egypt to vie for life in the desert.

Part II: The Exodus

We can get into the exodus now that the twelve plagues are no longer a mystery. As we saw above, people fled the Nile delta due to the sickness, the deaths, the poor living conditions, the political and religious climate was unsavory. The business must have been absolutely dreadful due to the afflictions and suffering of the people, the poor crops, the sick animals, and the weather after the Santorini eruption. Goodbye Egypt, hello world.

Our fictitious Moses (and please note that in the Egyptian language the words Mose, Moses, and Mes can all mean "son") leads a mass of 600,000 people out of Egypt and into the desert. The Pharaoh's army supposedly pursues the fleeing people and chases them to the shores of the Red Sea. We must ask why, if Pharaoh had decided to let the people go free why would he send his army after them? The Torah would have you believe that God put the fleeing Hyksos people back in harm's way and baited an encamped Egyptian army as they fled Egypt. To show the people that this was God's will, God wanted to prove to the people that He was Lord, and would keep them safe. Again, a perfect being needs to prove itself?

As the story goes, Moses leads the people to the shores of the Red Sea, and parts the waters with his staff. The people make it through the parted waters, but when the Egyptians try and pursue the sea closes, thus killing the army and proving to the people that God is Lord. Well, the first way to set this straight this is that we now know the words of the bible are wrong. Moses supposedly wrote the Torah, as inspired by God and the events of the times. When correctly translated, God led Moses to the Reed Sea and *not* the Red Sea. The Reed Sea, or Yam Suph as in the Torah, means Sea of Reeds, and was a body of water close to by the Red Sea. It has since dried up because of the formation of the Suez Canal. In Pharaoh's day, however, this shallow sea was a brackish, swampy area, filled with sea weed and, most notably, reeds. According to Occam's Razor, the easiest explanation is that our 600,000 people (if that number is accurate, and I highly doubt that it is) came upon the Reed Sea at low tide, and were able to cross. When high tide returned the Egyptian army that was pursuing them—for whatever reason—would not have been able to cross.

A recent and hugely important revelation sheds new light on the eruption and the exodus. Fossilized ash and magma have been found in the Nile delta that are from the Santorini volcano, and have been carbon-dated to the time of the eruption. To paraphrase Gil Grissom from the television show CSI, "Evidence does not lie. It has no agenda. It is what it is, and shows us what is whether we like it or not."

A better explanation lies with the Santorini eruption. The blast and subsequent tsunami generated would have made waves that slammed into the West African coastline at hundreds of miles per hour. At the time of impact the waves would have been at a height of six to ten feet. This event would have caused both the shorelines and immediate areas of the Red Sea and the Reed Sea damage. The Red Sea would have flooded inland, and the Reed Sea would have completely receded until the event had run its course. Such an occurrence would indeed be recalled with awe by ancient people and added/assimilated into tales and myth. Is it so hard to see that ancient natural disasters had such a huge impact on people who knew nothing about science? Well, for a blindly religious person, it is hard to see past fear and superstition. Step outside the circle of ingrained fear and superstition and see the world for what it is and the picture becomes much clearer.

Part III

Science and technology have shown the plagues and the exodus to be nothing but amalgams of natural disasters and embellished fancy. Mathematics, possibly the greatest of all sciences, will back up these claims, because the numbers just do not add up.

If I take, say, 1,000 buddies, and travel the desert for forty years it will leave a mark. Our passage will leave an impact. You will find evidence of our passing in many ways:

- The bones and bodies of those who died on the trek
- The bones and bodies of any animals we brought along with us
- Fossilized (or like) feces
- Remains of shelters, man-made or tents we brought along
- Remnants of our daily necessities, like weapons, pottery, nets, tools, etc…

There would be tell-tale signs of our passing. Imagine more than half a million people, plus livestock, plus pets. These people may have fled or may have left on their own, but they would not go empty handed; some would, invariably, have taken pottery, cooking utensils, weapons, farming and building tools, nets, saddles, wood and fabrics for shelter building, nails, extra clothing, and more. Do not forget food and water. The bible says that God supplied food in the form of manna. Manna, a magical food, rained down each day from heaven and nourished the people. That is as likely as the same people finding a Wendy's or a Popeye's Fried Chicken along the way as they trekked about.

Can you imagine the amount of food and water needed on a daily basis to nourish 600,000 people? It would take several freight train cars full of food and water each day to do so, and the desert does not support such numbers in terms of resources. Just as the world is not 6,000 years old, men cannot live in the belly of fish for days on end, and animals cannot talk, so too, does food not rain down from the sky.

Even if it did, what of all the feces the people would have passed? Did manna not make one go to the bathroom? What of all the bones of the humans and animals that died? There is no archeological evidence to support an exodus of more than a half million people plus animals. No bones, no feces, no tools, no trinkets, no graves. Again, Occam's razor comes into play, and the most likely solution is that a mass exodus did not occur. Perhaps many people left Egypt in steady streams, perhaps a few thousand left at once. Either way it is evident they did not wander for forty years. It is possible that people making an exodus from Egypt found a home sooner than forty years. It may have taken but forty days.

"It appears to me (whether rightly or wrongly) that direct arguments against Christianity and theism produce hardly any effect on the public; and freedom of thought is best promoted by the gradual illumination of men's minds which follows from the advance of science."
Charles Darwin, 1809-1882

The most likely scenario is that Egypt had become a terrible place to live. Its economy was in ruins due to the plague-like effects of the Santorini eruption, there was little food and too much disease, and if the political situation was not favorable to non-citizens then an exodus of sorts would be called for. The seeds of Amenhotep IV's monotheistic ways were already planted, the tales and stories from surrounding and flourishing religions fresh in the collective mind, and the time was right for such influences to create a new empire and a new religion. Enter the Jewish people.

It is obvious that these new people, the Jews, were the product of the last 3,000 years or so (BC) of life in the Nile delta. Between Egypt, Persia, Mesopotamia, and Greece there was a bounty of religions and cultural ways to plagiarize, yet the Jewish people did so very poorly. They are only partly to blame, for ancient man was so superstitious that it was hard to break away from old traditions and old fears—hence why the world still has so many people clinging to the Jewish and Christian faiths. They tried to break away from the sway Egypt had, and did make some obvious differences in their new religion.

The Egyptians had a knack for giving their gods traits of both humans and animals. They revered beasts, prayed to icons and idols, made numerous religious symbols, and even gave the stars human traits. Judaism forbid all of this, and did break away from such religious ways. The Romans, too, despised revering beasts, and not a single god of their great pantheon had an animal head or animal parts.

"Should we cover our heads and whimper because reality is not as we would have it? Beautiful lies are not superior to horrible truths, so why not hear the truth even when it is vulgar?"
Matt Berry

"Theology created the fiction of Satan which represents the revolt if an infinite being against the existence of an absolute infinity, against God."
Mikhail A. Bakunine, 1814 – 1876

Nine: Location, Location, Location

A man dies and finds himself in Hell. He is greeted by none other than Satan Himself.
"What am I doing here? How can this be?" the man asks.

Satan replies, "You have died and have been sent to Hell, my good sir. Do you recall that time you took God's name in vain, or that time you had an impure thought about that cute, young girl at the check-out counter? Never mind that now; you are here."
The man blanches, but can do or say nothing. Satan goes on.

"Listen, all the demons that process new arrivals are busy. What say I take you on a personally-guided tour, hmmm?"

"Sure," the man says, and follows Satan.

"Very good," the Devil says. "Right this way."

As the two walk about the cavernous place, the stench of fire and brimstone a constant, and the screams echo off the walls from every direction. The two soon come to a door and enter it and find themselves in a long hallway with an immaculate tile floor. All down the corridor, set into the walls, are rooms without doors, with wide windows for viewing. As they pass the rooms, the man sees that the spaces are filled with suffering people. One room in particular has a dozen men suffering a terrible fate; their moans can be heard through the thick glass.

"Satan, why are those men suffering so?" the man asks.

"Oh, them," Satan says. "They are Christians who, like you, took God's name in vain."

The man pales, and feels sick, but Satan ushers him along and soon enough they come to another window. In the room more men and women are suffering, but much worse than the last room.

"And here, Satan? What have these people done?"

"Ahhh, them," the Devil smiles. "They are all Jews and Muslims who have eaten pork."

"But Jews don't believe in Hell," the man argues.
Satan only shrugs. The next room has people that are suffering worse than the last two rooms combined. "And what of them," asks the man.

Satan says, "Those are Catholics. All of them sinned in some way. That heavy-set man ate too much, and died of high cholesterol. That lady in the corner was rich but gave not a penny to charity. See that once-beautiful model? Well, she was too proud of her natural beauty."

The two pass some more windows and the man is so numb that he has settled and accepted his fate. Then they come to a window with a room full of people who are suffering beyond belief. The anguish is unbearable to listen to, the sights too much for the man's eyes, and he turns away, begging Satan to take him out of the hall. With a wave of his hand Satan makes the two disappear back into the entryway at the gates of Hell.

"My goodness, Satan; what did those people in that last room do to deserve such torture? Were they rapists, Pedophiles, Murderers?"

"Who, them? No, they were Presbyterians who ate their salads with the wrong fork."

Part I: In General

It is evident that, because of the so-called existence of Satan, God is neither kind, loving, nor is He omnipotent. Another age-old argument is that if Satan exists then God is not all-powerful. If Satan does exist and God *is* all-powerful, then He is ambivalent and not perfect. Never mind Hell, if Satan exists and God cannot rid the world of "evil", then what does that say about a perfect creator, let alone one full of "loving kindness" to quote the bible. As I stated before, Christianity is not a religion of morals, it is a religion of salvation. It is not about living a good life, but accepting that a God had a mortal son who died for your sins. It is about believing in this and only this, and upon the acceptance of this will your soul be saved. You can live a horrible, terrible, murderous, lecherous, and otherwise sinful life, yet be saved solely on the notion that you willfully and truthfully accept a mythical man who is the son of a mythical tyrant. That is not morals, but salvation. Let me put it another way...

Christianity espouses that people lead a good, decent God-fearing life. If they do, the reward is a form of immortality (apart from the living, physical world). This is basically untrue. It is untrue because the leading of a good, decent life garners no actual reward. What brings about your prize of immortality is believing in God, and that God turned Himself in His own son who then "died" for mankind's collective (past and future) "sins". This belief is what brings about immortality in God's realm of Heaven, not the leading of a good life. If you do not hold this belief, then your punishment is eternity in Hell, where you burn and are tortured forever with no respite. Bad deeds like murder, rape, theft, war, cruelty, child molestation, pale in comparison to simple non-belief. What would be great is that if Christianity espoused that you lead a good life, and be kind and tolerant and if not-- *then* you go to Hell. It still takes away your supposed free will to be a jerk, but nothing is perfect. As it stands, leading a horrible, despicable, inscrutable life is no problem as long as, before you die, you confess your bad deeds and accept that God exists, and that Jesus is His son and our savior. All one needs to do to be sent to the realm of Satan is not believe a certain way, making Christianity a cosmic case of words speak louder than actions.

Why would a perfect, loving creator create a figure such as Satan and the realm over which Satan rules? Why would a loving, benevolent, perfect creator who is omnipotent and omniscient have need to such a being and such a place? The answer is as clear as a fresh rain drop; God does not exist. If God knows the hearts of men, knows all things past, present, and future, what need does He have of such a being to exist? What role would a creature such as Satan serve—good cop, bad cop? There is no need to test the hearts of men if one knows what the results will be, as the bible claims God can do. If God must keep His subjects in a constant state of dread in order to be saved and cherished what then of an after-life in Heaven? If Hell is supposed to be a place of torment for all eternity, how does Heaven operate? I can only assume it is akin to Hell in that if an immortal soul exists and goes to reside in Heaven it will be an eternity of trepidation, anxiety, and servitude to the same deity that brandishes fear as His main weapon in deterring people from doing whatever it is He finds offensive.

Jews do not believe in Hell. There is heaven, or Eden, and there is not. There is the light and love of God and there is not. The God of the Jews is a pragmatic being; either you fear and love Him, constantly praise Him, kill for do Him and as He bids, or He washes His cosmic hands of you when you die. You do not get to go to heaven. You do not pass go and collect your $200.00. You just go away, turned into nothingness. We all know what the same God says once Jesus enters the picture. He does wash His hands of you, but in a very different and spiteful way….down you go; a one-way ticket to the lake of fire, and the realm of never-ending torture with no possibility of parole.

Many Christians will tell me when I speak with them about Heaven and Hell that the Hell of the bible is not real, and is but a metaphor. They say that "Hell" is simply the absence of God, as the person who lived a life in rejection of God, Jesus, and the Holy Spirit will not be blessed enough to spend eternity with them when their mortal life has ended. That, again, would be called heresy, and goes against every teaching of the Christian faith, and so I do not buy into that theory in the least.

The main reason that Christianity has lasted as long as it has can be summed up in one word: Hell. The fear of being sent to Hell has given such strength to such an openly-contradictory religion that it has stayed the test of time. Fear is the best way to control people, and Constantine did a number on the world when he and his gave us Satan and Hell. If not for Hell and the promise of eternal torment Christianity would have been snuffed out long ago. Before we get to yet another plagiarism, we need to explore the paradox that the men who wrote the New Testament created when they crafted Hell and its ruler. Little did they know—or did they know and just not care—that man would not always be so superstitious and unworldly, and would outgrow the old ways.

The paradox is twofold. The first is that the God of the Jews and Christians is supposed to be an omniscient, perfect God of goodness and kindness. Why would a perfect being such as God create evil? If, in His omniscient foresight, God created all that there is and ever will be, why create Satan and Hell? We have to rule out free will because God, supposedly, knows the hearts of men, created everything and knows everything that there is and ever will be. If God is transcendent and omniscient then nothing can or would surprise Him, free will becomes a non-factor and the whole notion of eternal torment seems like a folly. Is it God's folly or that of the men who crafted the bible?

If it is God's folly, the Christian religion falls apart; God is not omniscient, nor is He omnipotent. Another being (Satan) exists that God cannot overcome. God, a perfect, all-knowing being, is surprised by His creations when they do <u>anything</u>. He is also not kind or benevolent because of Hell, eternal punishment, and eternal suffering. Moreover, He created suffering, sin, vice, inequity, and all the bad along with all the good. How then can the same being get upset with us humans at His own handy-work? You would think that a being as omniscient as the bible touts God to be would not create us (or all of creation) in the first place.

"If I am right, then religious fundamentalists will not go to Heaven, because there is no Heaven. If they are right, then they will not go to Heaven, because they are hypocrites."
Isaac Asimov, 1920 – 1992

I equate Hell and eternal punishment in this way: I set out to make a movie. I design all the sets myself, do all the casting, write the script, make the costumes, create all the special effects, and so on. I do it all with no outside help whatsoever. I have some major problems with the actors and their ability but leave it be, cannot afford better effects and so I am stuck with crappy props, the lighting was horrible, and the film had so many setbacks that it took years to make. When it is all done, I sit down with my popcorn and soda and watch the movie. It is horrible. I hate it. The acting is lousy due to the poor choice of actors; the special effects are horrendous; the cinematography is lousy, and so forth. I then have the gall to get upset with all the actors, and I am surprised by how bad the film is.

Is this scenario not the same with God sending people to Hell? He made all of creation, and made us with obvious flaws (or gave us the flaw called free will) and then punishes us for having such flaws. The argument of "God does not send you to Hell, you bring it upon yourself" is useless. It is, at best, gun-to-the-head tactics, and at worst the work of a sadistic entity. God holds a gun to your head and tells you to believe in Him and Himself as His own Son or you go to Hell for eternal torment. God is not telling you to live the right way, do the right thing, and be a good person for those sakes, but to be saved from eternal torment you must believe a certain way.

The paradox in the case of Hell boils down to this: A being that is perfect in every possible way cannot be surprised, cannot have human emotions, and cannot want anything, be it praise or the salvation of a lone creation's supposed soul. A perfect being that is compassionate and just who sentences Its imperfect creations to eternal suffering is one paradox, and that such a being would suffer human emotions is the other. The only way, in such a case, for God to be God is that God must be an imperfect being, and we are some cosmic pietre dish. The other explanation is that God is a being of perfect evil and torment, and so He relishes sending people to Hell. The best answer is that God is not real, and Hell is not real.

A deity who sends it worshipers to a place of eternal suffering over a place of eternal bliss based on beliefs instead of the actions performed while alive is not rational. A person can be polite, never murder anyone, hold doors for people, give to charity, save a person's life, love his/her fellow man, but will go to a hell of fire and torment for simply not believing in a certain way. Conversely a person can be a rapist, a murder, a thief, never give to charity, promote hate, kill puppies, seduce young men and women, and be a terrible human being, but all he/she has to do is believe in God and Jesus and apologies with some sincerity and they can bypass the realm of eternal punishment. It goes to show what a farce the Christian religion is, how it holds no value on human life, only the salvation of some supposed human soul, and its deity is a dark, uncompassionate being.

If you really want to be critical and fair, God Himself belongs in Hell; God has broken many of The Ten Commandments.

- Thou shall not kill/murder: God has killed billions via His own hand, plagues, disease, wars, the demand for sacrifices, telling people to commit murder in His name for land rights, committing numerous acts of infanticide, natural disasters, and so on. How many people kill because "God told them to"?
- Thou shall not covet thy neighbor's property & wife: Was not Mary Joseph's wife? Did either of them have a say in the matter? How many men did God tell to go forth and kill so that they may take their lands, women, cattle, and riches?
- Thou shall not commit adultery: See above with Joseph and Mary.
- Thou shall not bear false witness: Sounds like "do not tell lies". God lies all throughout the bible, giving false promises, telling people that he will throw mountains into the sea if they only ask, promising victory in battle yet denying it.
- God tells us in the commandments that people should not make idols or bow down to idols and such that represent Him, yet Christians **kneel** before the images of Mary, Jesus, and the Cross routinely. Moreover, if we are not to make an idol from anything that is of the heavens above, of the earth, or of the sea (to paraphrase the Ten Commandments) then what can be said of Jesus? Did God not make Himself into an idol that we are to bow down to?

- Thou shall not steal: As with the coveting, how many times did God order, tell, and demand that people go out and kill another people to take their lands and goods and take their property? That is murder and theft. God and Jesus also denote how slavery should operate. Is not slavery theft of freedom?

Beyond this, allow me to digress to what the Catholics refer to as the seven deadly sins. Like the Ten Commandments, these seven ideological and socially unacceptable behaviors are to be avoided at all costs for a person to be considered holy, virtuous, and worthy of God's love and admittance into His kingdom. Lust. Gluttony. Greed. Sloth. Wrath. Envy. Pride. If you cross-reference these seven and very human behaviors/emotions with the Ten Commandments, you will see how the very being these sins are supposed to offend are perpetrated by Him.

You shall have no other gods before Me. That means that God wants you to pay homage to no other deity, no other force, and to follow no other religion. You must only pray and swear fealty to Him and Him alone. Undoubtedly that is not just gluttony, but pride/vanity, greed and envy all rolled up in one. For a deity to be so insecure that a mere mortal paying homage to another deity would cause such emotional duress and incur an eternal punishment invokes God committing the sin of wrath. Does God not command in the Old Testament that any people who follow other gods should be put to death—whole villages, including women and children?

Moving on to another commandment, *you shall not murder,* if you read any of the Old Testament you can see that it is rife with murder. Most all of this bloodthirstiness is either committed by God, or done at His behest. That would be breaking the sin of wrath. *You shall not commit adultery* and *you shall not covet your neighbor's wife*, are next. Does God not impregnate Mary, according to the texts? Is this not adultery? Mary was married to Joseph. Is this not coveting someone's wife, for whatever reason? That breaks the sin of envy, greed, and lust. *You shall not make wrongful use of the name of your God,* or do not take the Lord's name in vain. That, too, would be seen as prideful and/or vanity if the use of your name in a derogatory way is used by hotheaded and faulty, imperfect mortals incurs 'wrath'.

"If God kills, lies, cheats, discriminates, and otherwise behaves in a manner that puts the Mafia to shame, that's okay, he's God. He can do whatever he wants. Anyone who adheres to this philosophy has had his sense of morality, decency, justice and humanness warped beyond recognition by the very book that is supposedly preaching the opposite."
Dennis McKinsey

Part II: Go to Hell

"And I will execute vengeance in anger and fury upon the heathen, such as they have not heard."
God, as he said in the book of Micah 5:15

Hell does not sound fun; there are demons to torture and haunt you, the lake of flame does not seem too welcoming, and the fire and brimstone must make for awful conditions—imagine if you had asthma? I bet the food is horrible and the service is lacking. It does not sound like my idea of a fun place to be. Imagine the postcard: Hell, a fun place to visit, but I wouldn't want to live there. Well, billions and billions of people have been sent there by God and most of them for no good reason at all. The murderer and rapist I can see. The pedophile? Sure. How

73

about the two-year old deaf child? What about the thirty-five year old mongoloid? What of the fetus who dies in the womb for some reason? What about a good, decent, upstanding Jew, or a fine, caring, loving Hindi? What about the Indians in the Brazilian Rain Forest, or the Tribal members of some Papa New Guinea sect? All you have to do to anger this loving, kind, compassionate being is just not believe in Him or His son, Jesus. Even if you have never heard of Them (despite that God is transcendent, making Him at all places at any given time). You would think that God would have spread His gospel to the far reaches of the world by now, but I guess His visa expired, or immigration laws are too tough these days.

Infinite punishment for finite sins is paradoxical. Punishment for being imperfect when one is created that way is paradoxical. Eternal damnation for exercising the very free will one was created with is paradoxical. It is fear-mongering, and a most ingenious tool, but it is as transparent as glass. One only needs to set fear aside and put rational thinking in its place. The idea to scare people into faith was good, brilliant perhaps, but it is all that is holding the faith together it seems you must fear God in all ways, fear Satan, and fear judgment. Earning respect is one thing, but being a bully does not garner true respect. It is not moral to threaten lesser beings with death, plague, destruction, suffering, and eternal torment to garner their love and/or respect. You capture more flies with honey than with vinegar.

Part III: The Big Red Guy...no, not Santa Claus

"Is God willing to prevent evil, but not able? Then he is not omnipotent. Is he able, but not willing? Then he is malevolent. Is he both able and willing? Then whence cometh evil? Is he neither able nor willing?
Then why call him God?
Epicurus, 341 – 270 BC

(One must note when Epicurus lived. At that time in history Christianity and its tenets and characters were not around, so it must be assumed he is speaking of the Judeo God. (Satan was not yet invented.)

Satan. The Devil. The Bogey Man. Beelzebub. The Big Guy Downstairs. The Prince of Lies. Whatever you call Him, you may as well call Him a god. I call him a convenient scapegoat. He is supposed to be evil incarnate, all that is wicked and sinful in this world, the corrupter, the tempter. Funny, but by reading the bible, the Torah, the Book of Mormon, and almost all such texts you can say the same about God. God tempts and tests, God lies, God kills, God demands human and animal sacrifice. Are God and Satan one in the same? Is God playing some cosmic game—or worse, some cosmic joke—upon us? Are God and Satan business partners?

So many people feed me the line of "Satan's greatest trick is making men believe He is not real." I was born at night, but not last night. Satan is just a component of the glue that holds Christianity together, and that glue is called fear. Satan may have served the purposes of the Roman government well, but the obvious paradox He bares should stare us all in the face—those of us who are not superstitious, poor, over-taxed, and hungry Roman citizens of the empire, that is. How—why is a better question—does God not only tolerate Satan's existence, and why did He create it? God is the creator, and He created everyone and everything with His godly omniscience and foresight. Angels, unlike humans, were not given free will, so how did this debacle all come about?

74

"Let us enquire. Who, then, shall challenge the words? Why are they challenged and by whom? By those who call themselves the guardians of morality, and who are the constituted guardians of religion? Enquiry, it seems, suits not them. They have drawn the line, beyond which human reason shall not pass -- above which human virtue shall not aspire! All that is without their faith or above their rule, is immorality, is atheism, is -- I know not what."
Francis Wright, 1795 – 1852

It is time for history lesson number two. Ha-Satan is what the ancient Jews called Satan, though he was not the figure we all know and love today. Ha-Satan was an angel in God's court, and his name translates to "accuser" or to be "hostile". The word has Arabic and Semitic characteristics. More references to Ha-Satan can be found in the book of Job. In this book God asks Ha-Satan where He came from. (What, God does not know something? I thought He was all-knowing and created everything?) Ha-Satan replies that He was wandering the earth. Ha-Satan had a career, however, before he was the Ruler of Hell; he was the D.A. for God, and His duty was to test man's faith. If you back track to a previous chapter God (supposedly) knows the hearts of men, and is (supposedly) omniscient. Why would He need an angel to do such work? It is an easy puzzle to put together. The Romans, who would have been very influenced by Judaism, turned the myth of the "wandering" angel that was "the accuser" and the "hostile one" into a fallen one. Then a home was created for Him, and his title of Prince of Darkness bestowed. The sheep-like people of the time ate it up; hook, line, and sinker. Too afraid for their immortal souls to see beyond the immense lie, Satan became a tool for control.

Another lie of the bible is of Satan Himself. Most of us know the name Beelzebub, Lord of the Flies. Do you, however, know the origin of that name? Ba'al Zebub was a god of the Philistine people, people who lived in and about the time that our fictitious Moses came down from Mount Sinai with the Ten Commandments. Ba'al Zebub was sometimes represented by a great bull, and was called the Lord on High, the Lord High Prince, and the God of Those That Fly. How easily the name and the deity can be turned into something else by altering the name and its meaning a tad: Lord of things that fly to Lord of the Flies.

Now for the million dollar questions: Why would God create Satan? Why does God allow His continued existence? How did God not foresee all of this? Why did God create evil in the first place? Humdrum answers like "free will" and "if you do not know evil you cannot know good", or "God works in mysterious way", and other evasive answers that clearly do not cut the cake. They are childish attempts to excuse reason and rationality and are preserved by fear. It begs the question I asked earlier? Is God Satan? At the very least God needs Satan, and is dependent on Him. Could Satan have been God's will, as the all-knowing creator foresaw he needed a scapegoat and business partner? The easiest answer is that God and/or Satan do not exist.

We need to take a closer look at the impact that Satan has had on the people from His inception up until now. The Christian religion would have you believe that Satan is evil at its best, or worst, depending on how you look at it. What did Satan do to gain such a nasty reputation? Aside from all the negative propaganda, Satan's accomplishments do not add up to a hill of beans. Not even a grassy knoll—an ant hill, maybe, but nothing bigger. Satan's grand list of evil deeds consists of him tempting Eve to eat the apple, He tried to tempt Jesus when Jesus walked the desert, and he told mankind and Jesus to worship Him. I also believe there are nine deaths you can lay at Satan's cloven feet.

That is pretty much it. I may have missed a minor deed or two, but when you compare these deeds to the every-day bloodshed, violence, jealousy, demands of worship, plague spreading, rape-promoting, slavery-promoting deeds of God you need to wonder just who the bad guy is. In this light God *is* Satan; the embodiment of evil and lies and wickedness. God has put more fear in man than Satan could ever hope to, yet Satan is the scapegoat. Satan tempts and Satan lies, and Satan is pure evil and powerless before God. Then why is Satan still around? Why not just kick his fallen angel ass out of existence?

How many wars were fought in Satan's name?

How many times did the Torah and/or bible ask for a human or animal sacrifice in Satan's name?

How many people were burned at the stake in Satan's name?

How many cats were burned alive in Satan's name?

How many cities listed (in the Peneteuch and in the bible) were all ransacked, razed, conquered, and looted by Satan's demands?

How many first-born children did Satan kill?

How many slaves were taken in Satan's name?

Were the Dark Ages attributed to Satan as well, or to humans doing dark, inhumane deeds in the name of God?

Was the Inquisition done for Satan's glory, or for Gods? What about the Crusades?

When the Portuguese missionaries went through Asia and India with their rifles and bayonets, were they spreading Christianity in Satan's name or God's?

When the Spanish conquistadors came and made war on the native Americans/Mexicans and forced them to convert and then killed them, in whose name was it done?

Do Islamic suicide bombers act in the name of God or of Satan?

When the Confederates of Civil War era America used the bible as back-up to promote and keep in favor of slavery, did they do it by Satan's decree, or cite God and Jesus Christ as their example?

How many Satan worshipers have bombed abortion clinics?

How many Satan worshipers have protested and picketed gay rights parades, or the funerals of fallen U.S. soldiers?

How many Satan worshipers have stood on town greens and preached their hate and intolerance, and how many have walked through neighborhoods with their pathetic flyers and pamphlets forcing their religion upon you?

How many books, paintings, musical recordings were burned in Satan's name?

How many more examples do I need to give? The answer for each question above is a resounding *NONE*.

God is accountable for all of the above, and more. He is accountable for this because His hands are dirty with all of these crimes, but ultimately God is seen as the creator of all and the buck stops with Him.

I am not defending Satan because I follow or worship Him. I, of course, do not believe in Satan and find the whole idea of Satan absurd, but as his defense attorney for the time being, His foul deeds pale in comparison to Gods. In fact, according to the bible, Satan did not really do anything horrible aside from tempt a few people. The only way this entire scenario and the entire idea and identity of Satan makes any logical sense is: if God and Satan are either one in the same being (and God needs this duality in order to survive) thus making God a being of perfect evil as well as some good, or God and Satan are separate cosmic beings who have a symbiotic relationship.

If the god of Christianity is real, my only conclusion is that Satan is real, and is a creation of God, either incarnate or in theory. Without Satan, in whatever form Satan takes (real or metaphorical) God cannot exist as the deity He is without Satan. Without the scapegoat with red skin, barbed tail, and bat-like wings, without the fear of being tortured throughout eternity with no reprieve for mortal, finite sins, Christianity would already have faded as most all other religions before it have faded. The love for Jesus is not as strong as the fear of Satan, for if you do not love Jesus in the right ways, enough, or at all, Satan gets your immortal soul.

The most sensible and logical answer, of course, is that neither God nor Satan is real; good and evil are human expressions and not cosmic forces.

In the examples above, and as taken from the bible, if you of the Christian faith, you are better off worshiping the lesser of two evils, who happens to be Satan. As for the answers to the million dollar questions, if you said "because neither God nor Satan exist", you win. Your prize is breaking the veil of falseness held in place by fear. If you answered with any other reply, you have lost—no money, no prizes, and no version of the take-home game.

"The faults of which we ask you [God] the remittance, it is you who make us commit them; the traps of which we implore you to deliver us, it is you who has set them for us; and the Satan which surrounds us, this Satan, it is you."
Pierre-Joseph Proudhon, 1809 – 1865

Part IV: Heaven

A man's dog dies. This dog was his loyal, faithful companion for many years, and the man is broken-hearted when the dog sickens and passes. Several years later the man dies, and finds himself in the clouds, with bright lights all around, and he just knows that this is the afterlife. He then hears barking, and is overjoyed to see his dog running toward him! The two reunite and much petting and face-licking ensues.

"Jack!" the man says. "I've missed you so! All these years you've waited for me? Oh, it's so nice to see you again, buddy!"

With that the dog gets up and whines for his master to follow him. The man catches on, and follows his pet, and soon they end up at a giant set of ornate gates with a very bored-looking angel standing guard.

"Welcome to Heaven," the lack-luster angel says, and then points to the sign.

The sign reads: **No Dogs Allowed**.

"What?" asks the man. "No dogs? Jack was my loyal pal. He waited for me to pass, and now he cannot come to Heaven with me?"

The angel only shrugs. The man looks to his dog, and the dog seems to understand. With a sad last look, the dog gives his master's hand a final lick, and begins to pad away. The man watches the dog go, and the angel opens the gates.

"Sorry," the man says, "but you can close those gates. If he can't go in, I don't want to go in either," and with that he catches up with his dog.

When he does, the dog looks at him as if to smile.

"Come on, Jack. If Heaven won't let us in, we'll just wander around the ether, or find somewhere else."

With that the clouds part and the same angel appears, this time with a big smile and open arms, and even a Milk Bone for Jack.

"Come this way, you two. Heaven awaits," the angel ushers the man and his dog.

"But what about the sign?" the man asks.

"Oh, that?" the angel answers, "That was just a test to see if anyone would leave their best friend behind just to enter Heaven."

*****

Okay, that is a bit corny, but my best friend tells it a lot, and I do like it. No, I do not believe in the afterlife, or Heaven or Hell, but I just like it. Perhaps it is the sentiment. I embellished it a tiny bit, and I hope I told it with some justice.

*****

Heaven is God's kingdom, the realm where your soul goes when your mortal life is over—if God allows it. According to dogma, it's incredibly easy to get into this realm of light and angels, of fluffy clouds and all the beer and pretzels you can devour. All you have to do is believe. All you have to believe is that God is real and that a mortal version of Himself came to life and then died for the "sins" of all mankind. That's it. You do not need to be a good person, nor did you need to lead a good life while you were mortal. That much is evident. All you need to do is believe a certain way and your immortal soul is "saved". Conversely, you can be a wonderful person, a shining example of human potential, yet if you do not believe a certain way you get to burn in Hell for eternity.

If God needs mountains of praise from mortals when they are still mortal, could you imagine what life in the after-life must be like in heaven? Church or Synagogue twenty-three hours a day, forty-five minutes of warnings if you mess up in any way, and ten minutes to visit passed loved ones and strum harps, and five minutes of free time. It is just a guess, so do not hold me to it.

There is not much to say about heaven, but I envision places like in the fantasy films we see; a kingdom ruled by a tyrant, only this kingdom is sunny and fluffy and filled with cherubs and angels (some good, some bad). Apparently you enter via a tunnel of light: we need to de-mystify that age-old fable.

When the human brain dies, we know for a fact that the last of the five senses to stop receiving input are the eyes. When the brain begins to turn off like this, your lingering sense of sight fades and one does experience a sort of tunnel vision. Neurons fire between your eyes and dying brain, but the signals are weak and images are reduced to light and dark. As the sense of sight dies out, the "tunnel of light" closes in upon itself, and the last thing your optic nerve will register is what so many people have said over the ages about that bright light and the tunnel. This same phenomenon occurs under sedation, and science has shown it is no mystery, just chemistry.

Add to that a human's own fear of dying coupled with the ingrained belief in the after-life. A person spends their whole life hearing of heaven, God, the after-life, of bright lights, tunnels, and the pearly gates. This placebo becomes part of our psyche and our own little defense against the darkness of death. Do you not think this is what you want to see and experience rather than what is really happening in your brain? To think otherwise is nothing but fear and ego; fear of death and finality, and ego that a cosmic being cares about you and that the universe revolves around us humans.

78

"If there is a God who will damn his children forever, I would rather go to hell than to go to heaven and keep the society of such an infamous tyrant. I make my choice now. I despise that doctrine. It has covered the cheeks of this world with tears. It has polluted the hearts of children, and poisoned the imaginations of men. It has been a constant pain, a perpetual terror to every good man and woman and child. It has filled the good with horror and with fear; but it has had no effect upon the infamous and base. It has wrung the hearts of the tender, it has furrowed the cheeks of the good. This doctrine never should be preached again. What right have you, sir, Mr. clergyman, you, minister of the gospel to stand at the portals of the tomb, at the vestibule of eternity, and fill the future with horror and with fear? I do not believe this doctrine, neither do you. If you did, you could not sleep one moment. Any man who believes it, and has within his breast a decent, throbbing heart, will go insane. A man who believes that doctrine and does not go insane has the heart of a snake and the conscience of a hyena."
Robert Green Ingersoll, 1833 – 1899

Part V: The Soul Reason for Religion

"I have never seen the slightest scientific proof of the religious theories of heaven and hell, of future life for individuals, or of a personal God… My mind is incapable of conceiving such a thing as a soul. I may be in error, and man may have a soul; but I simply do not believe it."
Thomas Edison, 1847 – 1931

I am not going to give this topic too much thought. I personally do not believe in the concept of an immortal soul. That goes hand-in-hand with what I've said above about fear of death and ego. Humans are so afraid to die because death is so final. We need to believe that there is another life, there just has to be something else for us. Our ego tells us that we are meant for some higher purpose, and that this mortal life is a staging ground, a leaping off point, a test. I am sorry, but that is pure fancy.

I am not afraid to die. I do not *want* to die, but I fear no judgment, no Hell, and not the wrath of a vain god. I live by the creed that this life is all we have, and that there is no after-life, no purgatory, Eden, or Hell. As such, I live my life without fear, and ask myself how I can make the world a little better while I am in it. I can be kinder to my fellow man. I can hold doors for people. I can tolerate and even love people different than myself. I cannot hate someone just because they are black, or white, or Asian, or homosexual, or of a different belief system than myself. I can donate to charity and help those less fortunate when I can afford to do so. While I am in this life, I can do all that without fear of reprisal from a self-called jealous god. If everyone lived like that the world would be a nicer place.

"The arguments for immortality, weak when you take them one by one, are no more cogent when you take them together.. For my part, I cannot see how consciousness can persist when its physical basis has been destroyed, and I am too sure of the interconnection of my body and my mind to think that any survival of my consciousness apart from my body would be in any sense a survival of myself."
William Somerset Maugham, 1874 - 1965

Christopher Hitchens wrote a book about Mother Theresa, and he had a valid point about one of her anecdotes. It seems, while in Calcutta, or some foreign place, she was holding and hugging some poor leper. A man walked by and said something like, "I would not do that for all the money in the world," to which Mother Theresa replied, "Neither would I. I do it for the love of Christ." Mr. Hitchen's point was, in a nut shell, do it for the love of humanity, not to gain brownie points with a [fictitious] god. My take on it is similar, but I will go so far to say Mother Theresa held the leper out of fear; if she did not for the love of Jesus would she would be rejected as she tried to enter heaven? If she was not a Christian, would she have held that leper? If she were a Jew or an atheist or a Hindi, would she still feel compelled to hold that diseased person? I am not her, and cannot speak for her. Even if she was alive today and I had asked her that question, could I trust her answer?

To impress the point I have made several times, the Christian religion is all about the saving of some immortal soul. The plain truth is that no one really knows if the concept of an immortal human soul is real and true. There is no real way to measure or detect it that science has found. There are no video recordings of a soul leaving a body, or of one that has been captured posthumously roaming this plane. There is also no real way to disprove that we possess a soul. It comes down to rationality and reason. The burden of proof, as with God, is on the believer.

I have heard too many people, close friends included, that tell "true" tales of weighing people as they die. For some reason they weigh a bit less at the exact time of death, so that must the weight of the soul leaving the body. Do you know how insane that sounds, yet so many people believe it? If we do have a soul, it is an intangible object, a part of our consciousness, not some measurable thing. If we go on diets and lose weight, does our soul get weaker? What affects the weight of a soul? It is a ridiculous statement.

I will not get into ghosts and specters and the supernatural in this book, but when dealing with human (and animal) bodies and souls, we **must** take into consideration Einstein's theory of conservation of mass-energy, or the famous E=MC². It began with scientist Antoine Lavoisier who stated in 1775 that matter is neither created nor destroyed. Years later in 1842 when scientist Julius Robert Mayer toyed with thermodynamics he found that energy is neither created nor destroyed. Einstein put them together in 1907 to preserve his space in history by stating that since energy equals mass as a constant, the universe's total mass is a constant. All things are comprised of energy; only its density is relative, and energy cannot be created or destroyed, but can change forms.

Human bodies are just conduits of energy. We are made up of dense matter, as in flesh, bone, muscle, tissue, and water, yet we run on electro-chemical and hydrodynamic systems. When a human body dies, it does not disappear, it decomposes. The denser parts slowly decay (unless we are cremated) over years, and become part of the earth. The old biblical saying "ashes to ashes, dust to dust" is true in that sense. What then happens to the electricity and other energy of our bodies? Is that where our souls are housed? Is that what ghosts are—residual energy?

Energy just changes forms. If I take a twenty-ton tree and cut it up into ten pieces and then completely burn all the pieces, is the tree gone? No. It has become twenty tons of ashes and gases. The tree did not disappear from the universe, its matter changed forms into ash and gas. That ash and gas will be used by the universe to create other objects that require said building blocks.

So, when a human dies, the same process takes place. In that sense we are immortal creatures, as our atomic structures will go on and make new objects. Some may be animate, like trees and plants and flowers, and some may be inanimate, like gasses and rocks and such. Does this energy retain our brainwaves and consciousness? It would be ridiculous to assume so.

The bottom line is that the concept of a human soul is fancy and ego. We humans do not crave death, rather we fear it. We are dying since the day we are born, and the idea of an immortal soul is the only war we can wage against the absolute certainty of death. Perhaps it is not a war, but the idea of a soul is the only ammo we humans can use in the battle. We will not go into that dark night, at least not without a fight and not without hope. Hope and fear and belief, in the end, are irrelevant. Death is the great unifier; rich or poor, famous or not, black or white, democrat or republican, saint or sinner, man or animal, we all die. Death is like the Borg from Star Trek. We will all be assimilated, and resistance is futile.

"Where is the soul? . . . I refuse to believe anything of that kind without proof. The idea that, as soon as a man's breath leaves his body, the soul flops out like a chicken's head and flies off into space to find a lodgment where there [are] harps and haloes.
Too much for me."
Robert Green Ingersoll, 1833 - 1899

"Experts in ancient Greek culture say that people back then didn't see their thoughts as belonging to them. When ancient Greeks had a thought, it occurred to them as a god or goddess giving an order. Apollo was telling them to be brave. Athena was telling them to fall in love. Now people hear a commercial for sour cream potato chips and rush out to buy, but now they call this free will. At least the ancient Greeks were being honest."
Chuck Palahniuk, 1962 –

Ten: The Great Cop-out They Call Free Will

This will be a short chapter. The reason is that free will is just not worthy of lengthy discussion. Too many people make it too big of a deal, too confounding, and too blatantly cheesy. I have long called it the great cop-out of religion. Now I see it as just a joke. Free will itself is an illusion, a weak response that so many people give in robot-like fashion. The illusion is that people think a human needs free will to be content, and God gave us free will so we could do as we please. "If God had wanted slaves and robots, He would have made us so," is a common religious defense. God, however, created everything and hence made good and evil, and when two of His imperfect creations (Adam & Eve) chose incorrectly, evil and imperfection was introduced into God's perfect creation and He punished all humans. (But does the bible not tell us that God will not punish the sons for sins of the fathers?)

The paradox that undoes free will is that God is supposed to be a perfect being and He is capable of free will and being content, and, being omnipotent, can create anything He wishes. He can, therefore, create slaves or robots that have no free will that can still be content and happy and give Him praise. He did not though, and He created imperfect beings that are capable of using free will to ruin their own contentedness, and a perfect being would not do such a thing. Then again, a perfect being would not need praise nor feel human emotions.

Free will is a joke, if one believes in the all-knowing, all-powerful, and seeing One, who sets all in motion. From the biblical get-go, where God put two naked, innocent humans in a garden with a fine-looking apple tree but forbade them to eat from it (He may have well put John Dillinger in a fully-stocked bank that had no guards and no locks) up to today, free will is irrelevant. What a waste all life truly is if God's free will is real. From men and women who die needlessly from rape, murder, inane accidents, to people who are eaten by wild animals, innocent people who die in accidents caused by morons who are texting while driving a train, subway, ship, or bus to the couple who are lovingly married for more than five decades but the husband inadvertently runs his wife over and kills her while she directs him into a parking space at the store—that last one recently happened here in Massachusetts as I finish this book, in July of 2009. If God knows all of this will come to pass, and most all of the casualties are His loyal flock, yet God does nothing to change or halt the outcome, what good is God? Again, painfully again, the reason is that free will is a feel-good illusion, and God does not exist. As Forest Gump said, "Shit happens".

Free will is the excuse humans use to behave badly and blame another—namely Satan. No one takes responsibility, or at least nobody wants to. It is easier to pass the buck, and lay blame elsewhere.

"Everyone would like to behave like a pagan, with everyone else behaving like a Christian."
Albert Camus, 1913 – 1960

I have always believed that humans are not inherently good creatures. In fact I believe just the opposite; I believe humans are inherently apathetic and self-centered creatures. The right thing to do is always the hardest. It is easy to hate, and easy to fear. It is harder to love and tolerate. If I walk down the street and see an empty soda can lying on the sidewalk, it is harder for me to bend down, pick it up, and find a trash bin in which to dispose of the can. It is easier to just walk by it and let someone else pick it up and throw it away. This analogy transfers to all aspects of human life. It is easier to hate someone than to love someone. It is easier to fear something than to understand it. It is easier (and more comforting) to believe in myths and fairytales than to handle the truth, hence why religion is so popular. Religion is like comfort food; that yummy PB&J sandwich with tomato soup, or mom's meatloaf and mashed potatoes with gravy, or the feeling that some supreme being cares about you and your mundane-yet-eye-blink existence and has a special, eternal place for you some day.

Life is not easy, not by a long shot. It is not all our own fault, however, and there is someone we can blame, however non-corporeal. She is Mother Nature. The only seguway off the topic of religion will be here and now. I said before that there no longer is human nature, only human behavior. Some of our nature comes through now and then, but in base actions like sex-drive, and the will to live and not die. We mammals all share one bad apple, one downfall of our respective societies: males.

While I am a male of the species, I can recognize and concede this. Male mammals are all aggressive. We all have too much testosterone. It leads to violence and macho B.S., be you a bull, a bear, a gorilla, a chimp, a lion, or a homo-sapiens. It is what we males are bred for. We evolved to not only impregnate our female counterparts, but to kill for them, hunt for them, and protect them. It is always the males of the species [of mammals] that pose the problems. Have you ever heard of a rogue female bear killing other cubs, or a rogue female tiger eating other cubs? Ever seen a lioness travel about killing young lions, or female chimpanzees beating to death young males? It is always the males of the species, and females will only do so out of desperation, as in life-or-death due to drought and severe living conditions. The same applies to homo-sapiens; males are usually the aggressors. There are more men in prisons then women, there are more male serial killers and pedophiles, there is more male-instigated violence in the world, and more males are the sources of more woes and wars than women ever will be. The old saying of "can't live with 'em, can't live without 'em" should apply to us men.

Back to the topic at hand. Free will is not something divinely given. We humans do things. Some are good, some are bad. Some are horrendous. What we as a species are fond of doing is the wrong thing and blaming someone/something else, and conversely we do a good things and praise someone/something else. Religion only belittles our struggle against our own behavior (as well as our intelligence and our potential). Religious people are quick to praise anything at all that seems good or just or naturally wonderful as God's work and God's Love. These same people are quick to ignore or excuse anything bad or naturally terrible, and put it off to Satan, some other source of evil, or one of God's mysterious ways. As with all such excuses and venerations on behalf of a supreme being it only shows just how irrational such an excuse is, and how much fear and, dare I say it—stupidity—has taken over one's faculties. Good and wonderful things happen, and bad and terrible things happen. People can do great things, loving and marvelous things just the same as we can do indescribably horrible things. It is not a question of free will, but behavior and responsibility.

Most foul deeds and acts, however, can be traced to religious views and practices. The Mayan people used to sacrifice humans by the hundreds some days just to appease the Sun God. Christians used to burn people they "thought" were witches, or labeled as heretics because they did not believe a certain way. The Dark Ages are a prime example of such bad behavior done to appease a deity, when in truth they were done to appease man's own innate trend toward violence and power and assertion of dominance.

"Religion is an insult to human dignity. With or without it, you'd have good people doing good things and evil people doing bad things, but for good people to do bad things, it takes religion."
Steven Weinberg, 1933 -

"The scientist who yields anything to theology, however slight, is yielding to ignorance and false pretenses, and as certainly as if he granted that a horse-hair put into a bottle of water will turn into a snake."
Henry Loius Mencken, 1880 – 1956

Eleven: Darwin vs. Dogma

I would like to address the issue of evolution versus creation. In my eyes, it is a shame to call it the "theory of evolution". It should be, in fact, the reverse: it should be called evolution, and the subsequent "theory of creation." It is a hotbed of talk and theory for the sole reason that four syllables can destroy an entire religion. E-vo-lu-tion. That word puts fear into the minds and hearts of the religious. They may not admit it, they may down play it, or they may dismiss it altogether, but the reasons they do so are born of fear and ego.

I would say much, if not all, is ego. This much is evident in the way in which people cannot stand to be compared to the rest of the animal kingdom, let alone primates. The best example I can call to mind is not the untold numbers of people who screw their faces up when I mention the word evolution, or speak of how we came from primates, but my own lovely wife.

My wife is as non-religious as they come. She has her own, belief of a higher power of sorts, but she is the furthest from a religious person as you will find. We have been married over fifteen years, and I thought I knew my wife pretty well. A few months ago we were talking, and come to find out my wife actually does not believe in evolution, that we humans are descended from the primates. Her reasons are not biblical, and certainly not from a religious standpoint. Her reasons are that of her ego. "Came from apes? Me? Preposterous!" Not exactly her words, but her sentiments. Her human vanity and her ego will not allow herself to believe that humans are evolved monkeys. Her ego contradicts her beliefs and tells her that, despite that she has no interest, no love, and no inkling for any religion, even when her belief in a higher power/God is weak at best she cannot allow herself to believe that humans rose to the top of the food chain by natural selection.

"Scientific research confirms that humans are a link in the evolutionary life chain. There is no credible evidence for the existence of an immortal supernatural element. Our only life is here and now. Make it worthy of a moral person."
Keith S. Cornish

We know from whence we came. We know life began in the seas; it started out as bacteria flourishing by undersea thermal vents. It mutated and adapted into primitive life, and over eons became fish. The fish and the sea-going invertebrates made a daring attempt to find more food and escape predators and came ashore, and the rest is history. Or science. History and science, ok? The fish and other animals adapted to breathe air and became amphibians and insects. We know that primitive amphibians once ruled a plant-barren landscape. We know that these animals adapted to the world by evolving into reptiles. While that was happening sea-going plant life extended to the land as well, and used the over-abundant carbon dioxide in the air to transform the world and make it suitable for oxygen-breathing life. We know these reptiles then dominated the world, and evolved into dinosaurs. We know that, for millions of years, dinosaurs ruled the land (while reptiles kept their grip upon the skies and the seas) and more advanced and

smaller reptiles began to evolve mammal-like adaptations. We know that some of these primitive mammals returned to the seas and the rest adapted alongside the amazing dinosaurs. We know that whatever forces killed off the dinosaurs left an opening for the smaller, more-adapted mammals to survive and adapt further. We know that birds are the direct—direct—descendents of the dinosaurs. That's right—that KFC you munch on and Tom Turkey you eat at Thanksgiving are cousins of the mighty T-Rex, and I don't mean the English Invasion band. We know that mammals evolved, adapted further, and that primates became modern man.
Phew! We know a lot. What some choose to accept, however, is another matter. For the blindly religious people, or those not blessed (by nature) with great mental capacity, they fall back to the bible for all scientific reason and explanation. They do not and cannot reconcile truth, fact, and proven science with faith.

For another example, just look at man's best friend, and also look at the horse. Dogs, we now know, changed themselves from wolves into what we know call dogs all on their own, and did it to exploit man's use of trash. Back just a few centuries ago there were no pit bulls, Yorkshire Terriers, Golden Retrievers, or Doberman Pincers. Every single breed of domesticated dog was hand-tailored by man to get the desired traits and features in said animals. Wolves, in order to exploit the food left over by early homo-sapiens man, learned that if they were less imposing, and could get closer to fire-pits, garbage sites, and huts, and could get a free meal. The humans, seeing these less-aggressive wolves, ignored them, and so these less aggressive wolves bred, and passed on their traits to the next generation. Floppy ears and smaller muzzles scared humans less, so wolves changed, bred, and within the span of two or three human generations the first dogs appeared. Once man started interacting with the dogs, and domesticated them, he would learn later how to breed them himself and change them further.

The same is true with horses: the draft horse, quarter horse, Spanish and Arabian horses, Philly's and so on are not natural creatures. Mankind bred and tailored these animals to suit his needs and wants all from one species of horse. If man can create new forms of animals using selective breeding in only a hundred or so years why can't nature reproduce similar effects, and have new species spring up en masse? It has happened, and it is called the evolutionary process, only it took millions upon millions upon millions of years and happened all on its own.

I suggest that man's own ego prohibits him/her from recognizing that, yes; we did evolve from lower life forms into a higher one. No, we were not divinely created. Our fragile human ego does not allow many people to believe that we were once primates. I see it as a tribute to the tenacity of life that we have evolved such.

"When I view all beings not as special creations, but as the lineal descendants of some few beings which lived long before the first bed of the Cambrian system was deposited, they seem to me to become ennobled"
Charles Darwin, 1809 -1882

Intelligent design or shoddy craftsmanship?

Our human bodies are designed all wrong. Nature is a wondrous thing, but she hindered us more than helped us when we evolved. We have too many defaults to have been divinely created. We have many spare parts, like the appendix, our vestigial tails, little toes, wisdom teeth, tonsils, just to name a few. We can easily live without them, and most of us have them removed—well, not the pinky toe, but it can be lived without in terms of balance. Our backs and knees are too weak to support our upright posture, and many people suffer from knee and back problems. You can count me among them, for at thirty-eight I have a bad back and have gone through a knee replacement, and am a cancer survivor.

Humans are also very prone to sickness, diseases, and it takes very little trauma to cause death. Is it signs of intelligent design that our limbs and joints fail so easily? Is it intelligent to give a created species so many allergies, diseases, sicknesses, and make it so easy to die? A mere slice upon a wrist can do us in, a few inches of water can drown us, it takes but a few pounds of pressure to snap a human neck, and a blood-clot smaller than the head of a pin is a killer, and this is evidence of intelligence in design?

The human body is a breeding ground and haven for the bacteria known as Staphylococcus, a leading source of death by self-bacterial infection. This past month I attended a course to re-certify myself for work in relation to safe food handling practices. The course is called ServeSafe, and is very informative. It teaches all about contamination, bacteria, infections, and toxins. As I sat through the eight-hour class, I was amazed by all the types of killer bacteria out there in nature. It takes so little of said bacteria to sicken or kill us humans while wild animals can withstand and even flourish on the same bacteria. Not only are there so many species of bacteria, many have come into existence solely because of humans and our advancements. Strawberries, for example, can be contaminated by the water that irrigates them. Animal fecal matter gets into the water supply via the reservoirs and that same water is used to feed the plants. Every single plant and animal and food type on this world is a breeding ground for bacterial infections, most of which are terminal to humans, yet "lesser" animals can either shrug them off or outright thrive on them.

If all this is intelligent design it is nothing to boast of, and I am not impressed.

> *"Today the god hypothesis has ceased to be scientifically tenable ... and its abandonment often brings a deep sense of relief. Many people assert that this abandonment of the god hypothesis means the abandonment of all religion and all moral sanctions. This is simply not true. But it does mean, once our relief at jettisoning an outdated piece of ideological furniture is over, that we must construct something to take its place."*
> Sir Julian Huxley, 1887 – 1975

I had an epiphany one day while surfing the net for something. An article about women and nail polish blinked across my screen accompanied by an image of a woman's foot with painted toenails. I looked at the foot and said to myself, "Self, what purpose would toenails serve us had we been divinely created?" If humans were created by God what are the function of the toenails? For climbing? Um, I do not know about you, but when I was a child and climbed trees I never used my toenails to aid me. For defense? I do not recall any martial arts style that uses the toenail, nor have I heard stories of how, when attacked, a human will roll on its back and brandish the toenail. For traction while running? Is that not the lower parts of the foot, like the heel and ball and toes, are for? Do we dig with them? Have we, as homo-sapiens, used our toes as digging tools? No, again. What then are toenails for? Why would a perfect being create creatures with body parts that serve no function other than to be trimmed and painted?

The reason is that humans were not created divinely, and that we evolved from four-legged animals into two-legged ones. We *used* to use the toenails when they were claws for all of the things mentioned above—climbing, defense, traction, digging, scratching an itch, but we had four feet then, not two hands and two feet.

In nature, and in man-made objects, form always follows function. It is why sharks are not square and are among the most aqua-dynamic as well as aerodynamic shapes on Earth. It is why chimneys are made to funnel smoke up and out. Since form always follows function, a divinely-created being would have not a single need for toenails, and a divine being would not craft beings such as humans with toenails. The mighty toenail brings the idea that we were created by a god crashing down. No wonder we prim and primp and paint and adorn them so; they deserve it!

The beauty of the evolutionary process is that is it proven beyond a shadow of a doubt; whether one chooses to accept it or not is immaterial. It is a fact of life and no amount of denial or holding your hands over your ears like a five-year old who does not want the truth can make the evolutionary process go away. No god can defeat it; no religion can stand up to it. The only way religious people can reconcile what they know is B.S. when compared to their religion's particular "Genesis" story is to make more excuses and turn off their brains.

No, dinosaurs and ancient sea-going reptiles did not live amongst mammals and humans. No, the dinosaurs were not all wiped out in the biblical flood story (and even if they were killed in a flood what about the myriad of ancient sea-going reptiles? They would thrive during such a flood, what with all the carrion and food to gorge on). No, dinosaurs and extinct mammals did not have their bones mixed with those animals that died in the biblical flood story. Show the biblical evidence to support any of these lame fantasies. Cite a verse about apatosaurus, nothrosaurus, pteranadon, velociraptor, tyrannosaurs rex, ankylosaurus, archaeopteryx, or smilodon. Show where in the Peneteuch Moses goes to sacrifice a hyenodon, a wooly mammoth, or a giant sloth. Why did Noah not bring any such beasties on his ark? I can tell you why, and that is because dinosaurs and sea-going reptiles died out around 65,000,000 BC. Most of the now-extinct mammals like dire wolves, giant sloth, saber-toothed cats, terror birds, cave lions, giant bears, giant elk—most all of which did not thrive in the Nile delta—started dying off at the end of the last known ice age, or about 13,000 to 10,000 BC. Men were not recording history then outside of drawings on cave walls. Layers and strata in the earth show us when creatures lived and died, and even what natural disasters took place. Among that evidence is a lack of evidence for a global flood. The rocks and debris and bones in the strata look and prove it to be a naturally-formed timeline of our geographic world.

To interject a bit here, the ancient Greeks always made the heroes of their myths larger than life. They supposed they were titans, true giants among men. Their myths were backed up with the bones they would find embedded in the volcanic mountainsides of their Mediterranean landscape. When huge, fossilized bones would be dug up or exposed by natural means, the ancient Greeks unearthed them. They could not equate them to anything but their myths; unfortunately they were wrong. Over time, by natural causes like erosion and volcanic activity, smaller bones, like toes, tails, fingers, claws, wear away. Large bones are all that is left, and the large bones of all mammals look alike; they share symmetry. What the Greeks did not know was that mastodons and mammoths once roamed free over what is now Greece. The bones, crudely assembled the best ancient men knew how, would resemble a huge, misshapen human. The ivory tusks would have weathered away, but the rest would not. The older bones of carnivorous dinosaurs become dragons and serpents and hydras. The huge three-toed horses that grazed ancient Greek grasslands, called Hyperion, become centaurs.

To deviate one can also cite the coconut as another example of form following function and disproving divine creation. What other seed on the planet is as tough, durable, and nigh invulnerable? What reason would a divine being create such a seed for? The coconut evolved its resilient outer husk not only to weather the tropical heat, but to make it able to float upon the waves as it crossed tropical inland seas when it was shed. The milk is an oily byproduct to keep the seed moist and ripe during the heat and on ocean voyages. Instead of this seed being proof of a divine being, it shows how the seed of the coconut tree adapted to the harsh life of tropical islands, and there are many varieties of such trees and seeds. A divine being would have little reason for creating numerous types and subtypes of coconut trees when but one type would suffice.

What scares Judeo-Christians so much about evolution is that if accepted, Judeo-Christianity instantly becomes high on the list of endangered species. It would be near impossible to gain any ground and crawl out of the corner modern science and thinking has backed all religions into. If things on earth can evolve, mindsets can evolve as well. When that happens, religions based on fear, ancient dogma, and intolerance become extinct.

> *"In the long run, nothing can withstand reason and experience, and the contradiction religion offers to both is palpable."*
> Sigmund Freud, 1856 – 1939

Lastly, I would like to call a witness to the stand. It is this witness that speaks on behalf of us non-believers, and is yet another reason that a benevolent creator does not exist. I would like to claim that this witness and its way of life was my own idea as to why such a creator is false, but after research I must concede the original concept to Mr. Charles Darwin.

Have you ever seen any of the *Alien* movies? I am partial to part II, *Aliens*, myself. The Xenomorphs are a scary bunch of critters; strong, intelligent, razor-sharp claws and tails, mouths full of needle teeth, black as pitch, acid for blood, able to stick to walls like insects, fast as a whip, grows from pupae to adult in under an hour. Most of all, remember how they bred? Do you recall how they gave birth?

Without further ado, I call a wasp to the witness stand—no, not a white *Anglo*-Saxon Protestant, the insect, *Hymenoptera Apocrita.* Ms. Apocrita, please raise your three right hands and repeat after me....

"So, Ms. Apocrita, for the record, please tell the court who and what you are."

"Of course. I am a wasp, a member of the insect family Hymenoptera, and we are neither ants nor bees, but an evolved form of hornet."

"Thank you. I would like to skip all the small talk and get to the heart of the matter. Tell me, Ms. Apocrita, how do most wasps procreate?"

"That is quite a personal question, is it not?"

"I remind you, Ms. Apocrita, you are under oath. You are not the one on trial here. Please, answer the question."

"Very well. Most all wasps are parasitic. We hunt mainly spiders and caterpillars to birth our young pupae."

"Could you be a little more detailed?"

"Well, we start by digging holes in the ground, or using smaller one in trees and under rocks. When the nest is ready, we seek out other insects, mostly spiders and hapless caterpillars. We, at times, have been known to capture reptiles, amphibians, and even tiny birds and mammals. We sting our victims, and the venom we produce is a special type of neurotoxin. The venom does not kill the victim, but will paralyze it for a long, long time. We drag the paralyzed victim into the nest, and then inject our eggs into the host. Over time the eggs will hatch, and our pupae—our fully-carnivorous babies—will eat their way out of the paralyzed host."

"I see. That does not sound too pleasant."

"Not for the host creature, no. Did you ever see any of the *Alien* movies? Oh, how we wasps love them. We always root for the aliens, of course."

"Thank you; that will be all, Ms. Apocrita. You may step down."

*****

If you can tell me with a straight face and no excuses that a kind, benevolent creator exists who made even one species that broods it young in such a manner, please do so. What a horrible way to die, even for an insect. I know we humans have little care for how the wasp breeds, but animals are innocent in terms of sin. Why would a caring creator create an animal that breeds such as the wasp does? If God is the perfect creator, and made all the animals, why would He be so cruel to other insects, spiders, and so forth by creating the wasp? Are spiders and caterpillars born sinners, too? What could possibly be the reason?

The reason is that the wasp, like all life in the universe, evolved naturally. There are other creatures in nature that reproduce as the wasp does. Why? Because nature is apathetic, and life will do what it must to survive. Gods are not real, and gods did not create life.

"The scientist who yields anything to theology, however slight, is yielding to ignorance and false pretenses, and as certainly as if he granted that a horse-hair put into a bottle of water will turn into a snake."
Henry Loius Mencken, 1880 – 1956

Twelve: Of Sheppard and Sheep

The words above are from, if you did not know better, L. Ron Hubbard, the science fiction writer-turned religious fanatic. He made an empire, created a religion, and became a wealthy, powerful man because of it. As you can tell by his own words, it is hard to believe if Mr. Hubbard truly believed what he was preaching or if he was caught up in his own lies. I do not wish to incur the wrath of Tom Cruise or John Travolta, so I will not pick on Scientology. I don't have to; it does that to itself. But the premise here is power and control. There is no better way than to control people than religion. Hitler was akin to Mr. Hubbard, but in a maniacal, genocidal way. Hilter, too, created a religion and induced thousands upon thousands of people to believe in it. Had Nazi Germany won the war, we'd not only sprechen deutsch, but we'd be praying to pagan gods. Hubbard did the same thing, only his religion does not tell people to practice genocide, like Hitler's, Moses', and Christ's.

It is ironic that clergy are often referred to as Sheppard's. People who follow clergy are often referred to a flock, just as sheep are referred to. Sheep blindly follow a leader, and will do whatever their leader orders and does. Who better to have wool over their eyes than sheep? Talk about a convenient metaphor.

"The King of France is called the Most Christian King, but this does him an injustice, for he never did a Christian thing... The Pope is called His Holiness but he is the biggest scoundrel on earth."
Maximilian, I Roman emperor and German king, 1459 - 1519

Many rabbis, priests, pastors, deacons, etc... are decent people. Not all are bad and poisonous, but many are. Many care not for the rhetoric they spew, but rather enjoy the power and the control, and, in some cases, the money. Evangelical preachers top the list here. There are so many of these people running amok, plying their trade, and abusing their hold over people it makes you wonder just how intelligent of a species we are? It seems, in the old days, God deemed to speak to but a few chosen mortals. Now, however, it seems anyone can hold a bible in one hand, a microphone in the other, and claim to speak on behalf of God. When I say speak, I mean speak for God, as if God talks directly to them. What makes them so special? Just because they have more charisma than others, or a better speaking voice, or more money they get special treatment from God? Why does not God speak to everyone in the same way? Why does God need these shysters to relay His message, and why is money always involved? Well, that last part is easy; religion is a business.

"What is the function that a clergyman performs in the world? Answer: he gets his living by assuring idiots that he can save them from an imaginary hell. It's a business almost indistinguishable from that of a seller of snake-oil for rheumatism."
Henry Loius Mencken, 1880 – 1956

Just like any other business, you need a profit in order to stay in business. Keep the faithful fearful, keep them wanting, and keep the collection plate moving. I suppose it is a high to be in power, to have hundreds, thousands, even millions, of people under your thrall. The money is good, too. People look up to clergy as if they are a different breed and class of human being, and that because there are a "holy" man/woman it makes them smarter, better, wiser, and worldlier. That, of course, is bunk. There are plenty of nice, decent, humane clergy out there, but there are also some polar opposites. The Catholic Church is ripe with them, and there are too many clergy that seek power, notoriety, and money. Look at the fancy sets and studios that the big-time evangelicals work out of. Look at the suits these people wear, the cars they drive, the homes they live in, and the television networks they sponsor. Look at the poor sheep in their audiences, crying, closing their eyes and swaying like reeds in a breeze, and throwing their money away for "salvation".

There is a church where I live, and it is a small affair. It was started by a man who came to America from South America with a dream. This man, this clergy, started a small church in my town, and soon had a small yet devoted flock of his native people. His evangelical Baptist church soon afforded him a shiny new Mercedes Benz, a large home with a bowling alley and movie theater built in, and a sail boat. All this the man needed because "Jesus" had spoken to him, and said that the man should have these things. The congregation joyfully paid for all of it, tossing their hard-earned money to their pastor.

"Remember there is a big difference between kneeling down and bending over"
Frank Zappa, 1940 - 1993

This clergy had so much control over his flock that he told them what and what not to eat, if or if not to smoke and drink, what sort of cars they were to buy, and who to socialize with. How do I know all of this? One of his flock "escaped", broke the bond when her checkbook ran dry, and came to work at my place of business. She expressed her resentment at herself for being so blind, that if she wanted a relationship with God—she had come to understand—that she did not need anyone's help. She is still a religious person, only now she does not attend any special church; she does her own thing in her own private way.

Look at these religious people on television. Look at these clergy and their followers as they rant and rave. There are entire television networks devoted to spreading religion. People by the thousands pack these auditorium-like sets, and millions more at home watch. They all send money in to further the cause, and to make reservations for heaven, as if money can buy you into God's kingdom. I never knew heaven had a cover charge. I hope you at least get free drinks and some peanuts.

"Marvel at his tricks, need your Sunday fix. Blind devotion came, rotting your brain. Chain, chain, join the endless chain, taken by his glamour. Fame, fame, infection is the game, stinking drunk with power, we see…Time for lust, time for lie, time to kiss your life goodbye, Send me money, send me green, Heaven you will meet, make a contribution, and you'll get a better seat…"
Metallica, *Leper Messiah*, 1984

You have to wonder how many of these television preachers believe in the stuff they spew. Do they begin as men and women with the love of God in their hearts and then get turned by the power and greed? Do they go into this business of salvation with mal intent, knowing people are sheep and will do anything out of fear or for a sense of belonging? Do they get caught up in their own lies and deceit, drunk with the power and the money? That last one seems to be a given.

Why would God need clergy anyway? Is God not all-powerful? Free will aside, if God is, well, God, what need has He of imperfect creations spreading His perfect word (even though we know that His words are not perfect)? You would think that if God wanted attention, endless praise, and blind devotion and wanted to instill in us free will, He would just make His presence and His words and His laws known. We humans could be born with all such knowledge of God, heaven, hell, salvation—or we could learn it from God Himself—and choose our own beliefs with our free will.

There are tribes in Borneo, South America, Fiji, and many other places that have never heard of God, the Christian faith, or of Jesus Christ. Why is that? If God is the one, true deity, why has not the entire planet heard? If God needs priests and rabbis and pastors and vicars and deacons and missionaries and so on to spread the holy word, how omnipotent is God? If, then, God's message is not globally known because His chosen messengers (the clergy) have not gotten around to every street corner and every jungle hut to at least express the holy word, can such people be condemned to Hell? Is it their fault?

> *An Inuit hunter asked the local missionary priest:*
> *"If I did not know about God and sin, would I go to hell?"*
> *"No," said the priest, "not if you did not know."*
> *"Then why," asked the Inuit earnestly, "did you tell me?"*
> Annie Dillard, 1945 -

Why is eating meat on a certain day of the week a no-no? Why must it be seafood on certain Fridays? This is not divine law, but a church-enforced edict. There are many theories, and most make sense in a stone-age mindset way. Here are my two rusted coppers…

Fishermen were not tithing the church enough. Perhaps their sales were down because there was a surplus of cattle or wild game. In order to get more tithing from the fisher folk, they needed to sell more fish. What better way than to have it canonized that meat should be prohibited certain days and/or certain times of the year? This is speculation, of course, but it is feasible, is it not? The bottom line is that the church is mandating what you can eat, as if it is some unforgivable act to eat one of God's own creations, using our free will to choose what we stuff into our bellies. God seems to hate pigs, snakes, and rabbits. Why not make people eat only pork, snake, and hare on Fridays to lessen their populations? Jesus was offended by the nasty, evil fig tree. Why not make fig casserole mandatory to go along with that rabbit soufflé, or cobra shiskebab as further punishment for the fig tree population of the earth? Then, when we finally eat snakes, rabbits, pigs, and figs out of existence, God will be appeased.

> *"In every religion, there are those who would drape themselves in the mantle of belief and faith only to distort its most sacred teachings -- preaching intolerance and resorting to violence."*
> Hillary Clinton, 1947 –

Lastly, if you do not know the reason behind why Catholic priests cannot marry, let me inform you. Dating back to the year of 1545 and to the Council of Trent, it was widely known that celibacy for priests was a church law, and not a divine law. The church will argue that a priest's duty is to God first, and not to himself. It is more to the fact that if a priest married his home life could over run his church life. When you add a wife, children, a home, and all the expenses that come with a marriage, it is easy to see how a priest's time and heart can become divided. Also, any money owed to the priest, or power he held, could be funneled back into the church instead of given to a wife and/or children. Especially when priests used to be given lands, orchids, and money. Upon death the church wanted the return of these things, and did not want them to be inherited by women and offspring.

It is about control. Jesus Christ and the apostle Paul hint that celibacy is better, but it is not one of God's laws. It is a man-made rule to control the men in power. Control is ultimately what religion is. Religion controls the people that the ones *in control* deem to be lesser citizens, and keeps them as such so that said people can remain in control. Religion fools people with false promises, fancy stories handed down throughout the ages or out-right stolen from civilizations past, and pretty tales of immortality, yet it is about dominion and domination. If religion were about creeds and values and morals they would be much simpler, much more tolerant, and only a few would ever have needed to exist.

"Many argue that Christianity is "different" from other religions -- that it is primarily about love of one's fellow man. The Crusades, the Inquisition, Calvin's Geneva all prove that this is not the case. These events were pre-eminently about obedience to authority."
Dr. Andrew Bernstein

"The careful student of history will discover that Christianity has been of very little value in advancing civilization, but has done a great deal toward retarding it."
Matilda Joslyn Gage, 1826 – 1898

Thirteen: One Step Forward or Three Back?

How much has Judeo-Christianity held us back as a species? How many centuries ahead of ourselves would we be if men and women were not excommunicated, burned, tortured, mutilated, and outright killed for not sharing a religious view? How much further along would our technology and medicine be if not for the same reasons? How great would our capacity for the arts be? How many diseases would have been cured, and how many lives saved were it not for Christianity and its fear and intolerance of anything that goes against its claims? Christians pride themselves as people who preach love and tolerance, yet their religion has done very little for this world aside from cause grief for the masses. All charities and soup kitchens aside, they pale in comparison to medical and technological research.

Stem cell research, for one, could have been much more advanced than it is now, and a host of illnesses and diseases could have been prevented in our children. How many free thinkers and budding scientists were either stifled of executed (in the darker days of our history) because they chose science or the arts over God and Jesus Christ? Would we be planet-hopping and sharing martinis with Vulcans and Klingons? I doubt that, but maybe we would be closer. Our everyday life could be easier, our gas prices a little lower, our food a little more abundant, our children more healthy, and our lives enhanced and improved had religion not held us back so much.

You would think that God would want us alive longer, to have better, easier lives so that we could praise Him more. You would also think that God, who created all and knows all, could not be surprised by whatever we humans invent; it was already invented by God and only discovered by us. If so, what harm? How can God be offended by such actions, or is it another ridiculous divine double standard? Akin to free will, is God saying that He has created things like stem cell research, cloning, medicine and medical technology, poetry, and music, rock and roll, and break dancing, but we are not allowed to use them as we see fit in case we offend Him?

"We would be 1,500 years ahead if it hadn't been for the church dragging science back by its coattails and burning our best minds at the stake."
Catherine Fahringer, 1922 –

I am not sure about 1,500 years, but I do agree with the sentiment. Long before people in Salem, Massachusetts started burning people at the stake for supposed crimes against Christianity, the wonderful and piously devout people of Dark Ages England were committing the same crimes. As they burned heretics, heathens, and so-called witches and warlocks, they shot themselves in the foot, and may well have aided the Black Death as the plague swept through Europe, killing 25,000,000 people. How so?

As the feverishly religious mobs burned men, women, and children alive, or tortured them to death, they also killed cats. Cats were seen as evil trickster demons and part of Satan's ranks. They skulked and stalked, crept about graveyards and into homes. Their eyes shone in the dark, and they mewled at night. So these morons killed cats by the thousands, burning them alive to torture and purify them as they destroyed them. What these religious fools did not know was that the bubonic plague, the Black Death, was carried by rats and mice. These dirty little rodents were full of lice and fleas, and when the rodents came into contact with people, the fleas and lice spread. Much like mosquitoes spreading malaria and West Nile disease, these fleas and lice spread the plague. With not enough cats to catch, kill, and dispose of the vermin, the rodent population boomed, dooming millions. It is a sad era in our history that could have been lessened if people were not so superstitious and ready to kill in the name of God.

Who knows how many people could have been spared? Who knows what new ideas for science, the arts, or what free thinkers could have come out of such times? How would history have changed if not for the deaths of all those millions? We will never know, and it will haunt us forever. The blame does not rest solely on religion for this, but it was a big part of the problem.

"The philosophy of Atheism represents a concept of life without any metaphysical Beyond or Divine Regulator. It is the concept of an actual, real world with its liberating, expanding and beautifying possibilities, as against an unreal world, which, with itspirits, oracles, and mean contentment has kept humanity in helpless degradation."
Emma Goldman, 1869 – 1940

Part II: Heaven or Hell Hath No Fury Like a Woman Scorned

Women. Ahhhhh… just the word conjures images of flight and fancy, of love and lust, of soft skin, curves however one likes them, and the magic of a woman's silky touch. As a man, I adore women; their shape and their form, the way their hips sway when they walk, their womanly assets and attributes, the way they smell and doll themselves up (though the best ones need the least "dolling"). As a male of my species, I am programmed to admire all that, but I would never treat one bad out of anger or jealousy, nor would I treat them the way Judeo-Christianity teaches men how to behave toward women.

Throughout the ages, most religions have treated women like second-class creatures, property, or worse. Judeo-Christianity is among the lowest in how they regard women, and I find it outwardly incredible that more women of these two religions are not more vocal, rebellious, and cognitive of their plight. Instead of going on and on about this, I would like to fill this chapter with quotes from the more vociferous women of history, and what they had to say about the subject. There are so many to choose from, but I will pick the most meaningful to make my point.

"Religion is now the first obstacle to women's advancement. Religion pulls human beings backwards, it goes against science and progressiveness. Religion engulfs people with a fear of the supernatural. It bars people from laughing and never allows people to exercise their choice."
Taslima Nasrin, 1962 –

"It is a significant fact that, of all the Christian countries, in those where the church stands highest, and has most power, women rank lowest, and have fewest rights accorded them, whether of personal liberty or proprietary interest. This religion, and the Bible, require of woman everything, and give her nothing. They ask her support and her love, and repay her with

contempt and oppression… It is thought strange and particularly shocking by some persons for a woman to question the absolute correctness of the Bible. She is supposed to be able to go through this world with her eyes shut, and her mouth open wide enough to swallow Jonah and the Garden of Eden without making a wry face.
Of all human beings a woman should spurn the Bible first."
Helen H Gardener, 1853 - 1925

"For centuries the leaders of Christian thought spoke of women as a necessary evil, and the greatest saints of the Church are those who despise women the most.…This coarse and insulting way of regarding woman, as though they existed merely to be the safety-valves of men's passions, and that the best men were above the temptation of loving them, has been the source of unnumbered evils."
Annie Wood Besant, 1847 - 1933

"The Bible and the Church have been the greatest stumbling blocks in the way of women's emancipation….The Pentateuch makes woman a mere afterthought in creation; the author of sin; cursed in her maternity; a subject in marriage; and claims divine authority for this fourfold bondage, this wholesale desecration of the mothers of the race. While some admit that this invidious language of the Old Testament is disparaging to woman, they claim that the New Testament honors her. But the letters of the apostles to the churches, giving directions for the discipline of women, are equally invidious, as the following texts prove:
"Wives, obey your husbands. If you would know anything, ask your husbands at home. Let your women keep silence in the churches, with their heads covered. Let not your women usurp authority over the man, for as Christ is the head of the church so is the man the head of the woman. Man was prior in creation, the woman was of the man, therefore shall she be in subjection to him."
No symbols or metaphors can twist honor or dignity out of such sentiments. Here, in plain English, woman's position is as degraded as in the Old Testament."
Elizabeth Cady Stanton, 1815 – 1902

"The stronghold of the church has ever been the ignorance and degradation of women. Its control over woman in the two questions of marriage and education have given it keys of power more potent than those of Peter. With her uneducated, without civil or political rights, the church is sure of its authority; but once arouse woman to a disbelief in church teachings regarding her having brought sin into the world; once open to her all avenues of education, so that her teaching of the young in her charge will be a broader, more scientific character than in the past and the doom of the church is sealed."
Matilda Joslyn Gage, 1826 – 1898

The very word woman in the writings of the church fathers stood for the basest of temptations.… As women were lowered in the moral scale because of their identification with her at the very bottom of the pit, so they cannot rise themselves save as they succeed in lifting her with whose sins they are weighed."
Jane Addams, 1860 – 1935

Persistently leavening public opinion, in a grossly superstitious age, with the theological doctrine of popular preachers, that woman is a sex of superior wickedness and inferior mentality, could have but one general result throughout Christendom. Not only did it gradually create within women themselves a passion of self-depreciation, humility and a self-hatred which led thousands of them to slowly and persistently torture themselves until relieved by insanity or death, it planed within the minds of men a jealous hatred and superstitious horror of the natural powers of women, which ultimately culminated in a veritable crusade of ecclesiastics against womankind."
Ellen Battelle Dietrick, ? – 1896

"It is a conspicuous fact in our modern Christian society that as a result and accumulation of our patriarchal development, the woman does not belong to herself.... Man has made her a perpetual minor."
Francisco Ferrer, 1859 – 1909 (not a woman, but he makes a decent argument)

"Right now religion has the romantic aura of the forbidden -- Christ is cool. We need to bring it into the schools, which kids already hate, and associate it firmly with boredom, regulation, condescension, make-work and de facto segregation... Prayer in the schools will rid us of the bland no-offense ecumenism that is so infuriating to us anti-clericals: Oh, so now you say Jews didn't kill Christ -- a little on the late side, isn't it?"
Katha Pollitt, 1949 -

Fourteen: To Love One is to Hate Another?

Many people hate the Jews. Bold as that statement is, it is the truth. Anti-Semitism has never faded, never been weakened, and will never fade so long as Jews exist in this world. Even if Christianity crumbled and died out overnight and the Jews persevere a thousand years from now there would be anti-Semitism. That is not to say that all or only Christian people dislike Jews, but the stigmatism is ever-lasting.

The main source of anti-Semitism is, of course, Christianity. Islam is in second place here. Despite all the jokes about their big noses, greedy and penny-pinching ways (though the most greedy among us seem to be those that seek the pulpit and try and buy and sell Heaven and Hell, the ones that sell salvation, and those that do not live as they preach), and funny headwear, it boils down to that Jews are always seen as the killers of Jesus Christ. That fact will never die. Muslims and Jews are always cast as bitter rivals, and that source stems from the first Christian bibles back in Emperor Constantine I's time. It starts in Genesis where the sons of Abraham are debated and what their lives beheld. It continues in the Qu'ran where some parts tell practicing Muslims to treat Jews as "Brothers" and some parts tell practicing Muslims to attack Jews who will not convert to Islam. Later, the hatred was fueled by the Spaniards with the Inquisition and then most notably by Hitler with the Holocaust, and lately by people like Mel Gibson. There are so many reasons and theories why Hitler was an anti-Semite, but this book is just not long enough to delve into that, but the fact is that anti-Semitism has been around for roughly 2,000 years. The reason, ultimately, is simple: Jews (supposedly) killed Christ.

If you are a student of history, you will know the story of Christ. Regardless if Christ was a real person or a mythical being of pure allegory, the story of this god-man is not some divine secret. Most amazing is that nearly all practicing Christians seem to believe only what they want to when it comes to the death of their messiah. Yes Jesus was a Jew. Yes he was a radical in that he opposed Rome, opposed polytheism, claimed he was the son of God and God incarnate, and said He could work miracles. Yes He messed with Rome, its governing ways, it coffers, and its integrity. Yes the Jews at the time saw Christ as a rabble-rouser, and ultimately a blasphemer for His views and ways. Yes the Jews at the time would have killed Christ if the Romans had not. Yes the Romans were the ones who crucified Christ, and the Jews did not stop or hinder them.

Judaism preaches that anyone who follows a god that is not God should be killed, just as the Christian God demands, and just as the Muslim, Allah, demands. That these edicts are ignored by modern-day Jews and Christians is beside the point (and a damned good thing), can you blame the Jews for following their religious beliefs **and** keep in mind the state of men's mental faculties of 2,000 years ago?

As blood thirsty as the Norse gods were, the Viking religious edicts never have Odin telling the Norse to commit genocide. Ra and Zeus never command it, and neither do Brahma or even the horribly bloodthirsty Mayan and Aztec gods. Oh these gods loved war and mayhem, but it was not paramount to wipe out other races just because they believed in or followed other deities.

"Suppose, however, that God did give this law to the Jews, and did tell them that whenever a man preached a heresy, or proposed to worship any other God that they should kill him; and suppose that afterward this same God took upon himself flesh, and came to this very chosen people and taught a different religion, and that thereupon the Jews crucified him; I ask you, did he not reap exactly what he had sown? What right would this god have to complain of a crucifixion suffered in accordance with his own command?"
Robert Green Ingersoll, 1833 – 1899

No matter what the argument is, anti-Semitism boils down to that, according to the Christian Bible, the Jews killed Christ, and that is what has stuck through the ages. Here is my very odd thought on the subject: What if Christ was real and he had not been executed? What if he left the Holy Land and Roman territory before he could be tried and put to death? What if He was simply just not killed, and went on to preach and teach His ways? If that happened Christianity would never have come about. Christ never would have "died for our sins", and Heaven would be all but un-attainable. When you think on it that way, is not Christ's death the best possible thing to have happened? If He was not martyred, what then would have become of Him? Moreover, the death was not even real since Jesus supposedly arose three days later unscathed and ascended to Heaven.

"Now a Jew, in the dictionary, is one who is descended from the ancient tribes of Judea, or one who is regarded as descended from that tribe. That's what it says in the dictionary; but you and I know what a Jew is -- One Who Killed Our Lord… And although there should be a statute of limitations for that crime, it seems that those who neither have the actions nor the gait of Christians, pagan or not, will bust us out, unrelenting dues, for another deuce… Alright, let's admit it, we Jews killed Christ -- but it was only for three days."
Lenny Bruce, 1925 - 1966

Anne Rice wrote a wonderful book titled *Memnoch the Devil*. It is one of her Vampire Lestat novels, but I find it to be the most entertaining, most vivid, and most pensive of her works. I would love for you to get a copy and read it cover-to-cover, and do not want to ruin it if you have not read it, but Mrs. Rice has a great thought in the book. In a nut shell, Satan is speaking to Jesus. Satan says that He [Jesus/God] is going about this all wrong, and that He is missing the big picture. Satan tells Jesus/God that the whole living life as a mortal and dying for human sin is just back-assward, and that it is not being done in the correct fashion. The book is more about God, Satan, Heaven, and Hell than vampires and drinking mortal blood and all, and I highly suggest it as a read. It deals with religion, spirituality, even God-deemed evolution of the supernatural. If you get a chance, believer or non-believer, please read this book.

But people still hate the Jews. People love to hate. It is what we do best. The only other animal to really hate is the lion. Lions hate hyenas and will kill them whenever they get a chance. Most times they will kill them and leave their bodies to the scavengers, and other times a big male will kill a hyena and eat it even if he is full just to spite the hyena. When it comes to true hate, though, humans are king. Do not forget, either, that we humans are supposedly made in God's image, and God hates just as much as we do.

Funny how the Torah and the Bible claim that the Children of Israel, the Jews, are the chosen ones yet Jews are among the most hated people on the planet. What I find amusing is that while people that inwardly, outwardly, or both, hate Jews still do these following things: wear clothes and use products by Levis, Calvin Klein, Ralph Lauren, and other noted Jewish fashion and home goods merchants; see movies and shows staring Jews; listen to bands who are/feature Jews; read their novels, buy their art; benefit from Israel's medical sciences and never complain.

Christians seem to ignore the teachings of their messiah and the tenets of Christianity that preach forgiveness. If Jesus)Jew and rabbi) supposedly died for all of mankind's collective sins, would that not include the Jews as well? Since Jesus made this sacrifice, should not all hate and intolerance toward Jews end? No one hates the Romans or Italians, and they are the ones who crucified Christ.

No. What people recall and what people are taught is that Jews killed Christ. That is all that will ever be remembered. Such is the way of mankind; long is his memory for what is bad, and short for what is good.

Fifteen: Who, What, and Why?

Who are we? Why are we here? What is our purpose? The existential begs to be answered, but why make it so hard? Does it really matter how life came to be? Does it really matter why we are here? Do we as a species *really* need some grand purpose? Why do people of faith espouse that we need to have faith in order to see beyond the veil of what we do not and cannot yet understand? Religious defenders, God's defenders, say that faith in God is necessary to understand all that science cannot and can never show us. That is just a load of manure. Science is the most amazing tool at our disposal, along with our imagination. What we term as the God of the Gaps the religious try to term as Atheism of the Gaps. The religious feel some need to ignore science and rely on faith in its place. They put all these human emotions and human longings into existentialism. Their whole problem is their ego; big, fat, full-of themselves, I'm so important, God loves me, and we have a grand purpose ego!

Why are we here? How did life arise if not by the divine? My answer: who cares? What does it matter? If we did evolve out of cosmic pea soup coupled with chance and tribulation or if some "divine" force created us, does it change the fact that as a species we are failing miserably? Does it change the fact that we do terrible things to each other, war upon each other, hate each other, and that nothing looks like it will ever change? If divinely created with some higher purpose we are, what the heck is God waiting for? Tell us this grand scheme instead of letting us fumble about in the dark as we wipe our own species off the map. Stop sitting up there in Heaven with Your transcendent arms folded watching us makes fools out of ourselves.

To burst some egotistical bubbles, we are here because life will do what it must do to survive. We are evolved pond scum. We are here to procreate and make more evolved pond scum. We made our gods along the way, and we do not need them anymore.

Yes, science can show us everything. No, it cannot do so in a timely manner. Atheism of the Gaps is a lame attempt to pump life into a dying religion. No religion can withstand reason and science. No god can face reality because the reality is that there are no gods. One can anthropomorphize the universe all he or she likes, and argue that science cannot show us the way to spiritual bliss. I will agree to that last point, but I will say that religion cannot do that either. Living in fear of God, Hell, and judgment is not spiritual bliss. It is akin to spiritual torture. A human does not need God, or any religion, to live a happy, fulfilling life.

Humans do not need God; God needs humans. The religious always say that atheists hate God, and that they turn from Him because there are reasons of conscience that we atheists cannot equivocate. What the religious and pious always fail to see is that atheists cannot hate God—we do not believe in God. Hating God to an atheist is akin to hating Toucan Sam, or unicorns, or vampires. God is not real, Toucan Sam is not real. We people of no faith do not hate God, we reject the idea of God, of gods, and we do not bother with questions pertaining to the supernatural which have no answer and *never will*. These questions and these theologies have no meaning to us, and we do not concern ourselves with them. It is only important to those infected with the disease of religion that these matters pertain to, and mostly out of fear for their non-existent "immortal souls". If God is real, and is the perfect being that the bible says He is, do you really think the child-like mindset of humans can possibly confound or irritate Him? If it does, just what sort of perfect being are you paying homage to?

In the bible God Himself tells us that he is jealous and vain. Is that fact conveniently forgotten? That alone tells you that a being is not perfect. Atheists do not concern themselves with doing right by God and Jesus Christ. We concern ourselves with doing right by our fellow humans. We see the big picture, not the wallet-sized one that has a set of pearly gates on one side and a lake of fire on the other.

For whatever reason or happenstance, we are here because life arose. Be it chance, circumstance, and luck, divinely, or because little green men in flying saucers played chemistry lab, we are here. How life arose does not concern an atheist, but we as humans know beyond any reasonable doubt that we were not made from mud. Did the universe and all life within it have a divine spark? Atheists do not know and we do not care. It is irrelevant. The universe acts as if there were no God (even if there is) and we atheists and agnostics and secularists live life not concerning ourselves with such a trivial matter. As Darwin said, the issue of theology is "insoluble" to humans, and it should not be something that we waste lifetimes debating and warring over. Atheists are not evil, and we are not fanatical. We are humans who are not tethered by fear and lies, not burdened with guilt and not blindly accepting things as they are.

"The opposite of the religious fanatic is not the fanatical atheist but the gentle cynic who cares not whether there is a god or not."
Eric Hoffer, 1902- 1983

Is science the god of the atheist and agnostic? I cannot answer that save for my own opinion. If you want to name science a religion, then the answer would be "affirmative". If that is the case, this religion is infinitely superior to Judeo-Christianity. Science is not jealous or vain. Science does not crave human sacrifice, unless you count the time we humans sacrifice to explore and learn. Science does not cause floods or plagues to kill off entire races of beings. Science does not tell us to make war on other beings, take their lands and goods, rape their women, kill their children, how to keep and sell slaves, and raze villages. Science does not tell us that we will burn in some other-worldly hell if we do not believe in what we find. Science does not tell us to hate, kill, or not tolerate beings with a different mindset or religion. All of this the Judeo-Christian God demands, but all science wants is for us to learn and to discover. No wonder the religious fear science—it can kill gods.

"When the masses become better informed about science, they will feel less need for help form supernatural Higher Powers. The need for religion will end when man becomes sensible enough to govern himself."
Francisco Ferrer, 1859 – 1909

Religious people ask, what will it take for you [the non-believer] to believe? What would be considered proof? That question is irrelevant. My best answer is not mine. I had written a long answer during the draft of this book, but came across this post on the internet as I studied and looked for theories and ideas. It belongs to an internet user known only as Somber. I think that Somber's statement is quite eloquent, and a fitting way to end this chapter. He/She writes:

"What level of scientific evidence would be needed to prove the existence of such a being? To be honest, there are no scientific criteria I can imagine to apply to such a question. Neither religion nor metaphysics nor physics can conclusively define things such as what God is. Is God matter? Energy? Some other state of existence unknown? Quantum? Sub-quantum? And if God is such an esoteric and alien being then why is it that such a being needs or cares about human endeavors and behaviors? Is eating fish on Friday really so vital to such a transcendental creature? Is there any logical explanation for why rabbits are an abomination to it? These are questions that need to be presented by theists in order for them to even be applicable to science. If you presume God to exist then you should be able to posit some testable traits of such a being. If you cannot, it is not a failure of science. It is nothing more than the failing of your manufactured mythology unable to hold up to the cold and callous truth of the universe."

"A devout clergyman sought every opportunity to impress upon the mind of his son the fact that God takes care of all His creatures. Happening one day to see a crane wading in quest of food, the good man pointed out to his son the perfect adaptation of the crane to get his living in that manner. "See," said he, "how his legs are formed for wading! What a long slender bill he has! Observe how nicely he folds his feet when putting them in or drawing them out of the water! He does not cause the slightest ripple. He is thus enabled to approach the fish without giving them any notice of his arrival." "My son," said he, "it is impossible to look at that bird without recognizing the design, as well as the goodness of God, in thus providing the means of subsistence." "Yes," replied the boy, "I think I see the goodness of God, at least so far as the crane is concerned; but after all, father, don't you think the arrangement a little tough on the fish?"
Robert Green Ingersoll, 1833 - 1899

Fifteen: To Eat or not to Eat, That is the Question

I do not understand being kosher. I mean I know what it is and why, but I do not *understand* it. If God is real and made all the creatures on this world and made humans omnivores, why are certain animals not to be eaten? Moreover, why are some animals only allowed to be partially eaten? You can eat a cow's tongue, brain, liver, and heart, and selected cuts of meat, but not certain parts of the rest of its body? If, after Eve made her big mistake, humans and animals were to be mortal enemies (in some cases) why can we not eat all of them?

One of the edicts of being kosher is that only fish with scales may be eaten. This means no catfish, no shellfish, and no squid. Kosher people may not ingest any of these animals, but, if given the chance and or opportunity, these same animals would eat us (by way of us being carrion, and there are even huge, killer catfish in Indonesia that are known man-eaters). Swine are always a sign of an unclean animal, and are not kosher. Why do Christians—especially evangelicals and the orthodox—not keep kosher? Why did they move away from the culinary edicts of Judaism if Jesus was purportedly a Jew, a Rabbi, and must have kept kosher? In Hinduism special preference and reverence is placed on many animals because they have anthropomorphized these animals into gods, or more to the point, given their gods the attributes of both man and the animals they find interesting and reverent. Judaism prohibits such actions, yet certain animals are seen as unfit to eat. In the end, how can the act of eating an animal offend a being that is the apex of the cosmic food chain?

Kosher edicts come from the Hebrew Old Testament, where God describes to man what animals are clean and unclean. It starts in Genesis where God described to Noah what animals are worth saving, and which ones are not. In Leviticus it is further described what animals to eat and what animals or what parts of animals are unfit to eat. The men who wrote the bible liked the word abomination, and use it frequently. They also use the words unclean, and "detest". Many animals are deemed to be abominations, unclean, and detestable, so I ask again, why would God create abominations that are unclean and detestable?

If you did not know why people keep kosher, I will cite the verses that explain it in the eyes of biblical man. Pay close attention to the wording of the descriptions of the animals God deems worthy and unworthy. I will put in bold the passages that, to any thinking person, should stand out.

Leviticus 11: The LORD said to Moses and Aaron, "Say to the Israelites: 'Of all the animals that live on land, these are the ones you may eat: You may eat any animal that has a split hoof completely divided and that chews the cud; there are some that only chew the cud or only have a split hoof, but you must not eat them. The camel, though it chews the cud, does not have a split hoof; it is ceremonially unclean for you. The coney, though it chews the cud, does not have a split hoof; it is unclean for you. **The rabbit, though it chews the cud**, does not have a split hoof; it is unclean for you. And the pig, though it has a split hoof completely divided, does not chew the cud; it is unclean for you. You must not eat their meat or touch their carcasses; they are unclean for you. 'Of all the creatures living in the water of the seas and the streams, you may eat any that have fins and scales. But all creatures in the seas or streams that do not have fins and scales—whether among all the swarming things or among all the other living creatures in the water—you are to detest. And since you are to detest them, you must not eat their meat and you must detest their carcasses. Anything living in the water that does not have fins and scales is to be detestable to you. "These are the **birds** you are to detest and not eat because they are detestable: the eagle, the vulture, the black vulture, the red kite, any kind of black kite, any kind of raven, the horned owl, the screech owl, the gull, any kind of hawk, the little owl, the cormorant, the great owl, the white owl, the desert owl, the osprey, the stork, any kind of heron, the hoopoe **and the bat.**" **All flying insects that walk on all fours** are to be detestable to you. **There are, however, some winged creatures that walk on all fours** that you may eat: those that have jointed legs for hopping on the ground. Of these you may eat any kind of locust, katydid, cricket or grasshopper. **But all other winged creatures that have four legs** you are to detest. "You will make yourselves unclean by these; whoever touches their carcasses will be unclean till evening. Whoever picks up one of their carcasses must wash his clothes, and he will be unclean till evening. "Every animal that has a split hoof not completely divided or that does not chew the cud is unclean for you; whoever touches the carcass of any of them will be unclean. Of all the animals that walk on all fours, those that walk on their paws are unclean for you; whoever touches their carcasses will be unclean till evening. Anyone who picks up their carcasses must wash his clothes, and he will be unclean till evening. They are unclean for you. "'Of the animals that move about on the ground, these are unclean for you: the weasel, the rat, any kind of great lizard, the gecko, the monitor lizard, the wall lizard, the skink and the chameleon. Of all those that move along the ground, these are unclean for you. Whoever touches them when they are dead will be unclean till evening. When one of them dies and falls on something, that article, whatever its use, will be unclean, whether it is made of wood, cloth, hide or sackcloth. Put it in water; it will be unclean till evening, and then it will be clean. If one of them falls into a clay pot, everything in it will be unclean, and you must break the pot. Any food that could be eaten but has water on it from such a pot is unclean, and any liquid that could be drunk from it is unclean. Anything that one of their carcasses falls on becomes unclean; an oven or cooking pot must be broken up. They are unclean, and you are to regard them as unclean. A spring, however, or a cistern for collecting water remains clean, but anyone who touches one of these carcasses is unclean. If a carcass falls on any seeds that are to be planted, they remain clean. But if water has been put on the seed and a carcass falls on it, it is unclean for you. "'If an animal that you are allowed to eat dies, anyone who touches the carcass will be unclean till evening. Anyone who eats some of the carcass must wash his clothes, and he will be unclean till evening. Anyone who picks up the carcass must wash his clothes, and he will be unclean till evening. "'Every creature that moves about on the ground is detestable; it is not to be eaten. You are not to eat any creature that moves about on the ground, whether it moves on its belly or walks on all fours or on many feet; it is detestable. Do not defile yourselves by any of these creatures. Do not make yourselves unclean by means of them or be made unclean by them. I am the LORD your God; consecrate yourselves and be holy, because I am holy. Do not make yourselves unclean by any creature that moves about on the ground. I am the LORD who brought you up out of Egypt to be your God; therefore be holy, because I am holy. "These are the regulations concerning animals, birds, every living thing that moves in the water and every creature that moves about on the ground. You must distinguish between the unclean and the clean, between living creatures that may be eaten and those that may not be eaten. "

Leviticus 3:17 "It shall be a perpetual statute throughout your generations in all your dwellings, that you shall not eat either fat or blood."

Quite a mouthful and one you cannot make a meal of. There is more about animals in the bible, this time about which ones Noah can save from the flood. Also, twice in Exodus and once in Deuteronomy the Torah forbids the boiling of a kid in its mother's milk. No, not a human child, but a goat or lamb. This continues to cows and such, as these early people felt it cruel to kill a baby animal and cook it in its mother's milk. I can see the reasons for it when I look through their ancient eyes, and this is the reasons kosher people do not drink milk with meat. As for owls and eagles, how can anyone find them detestable? These two birds are some of the most noble-looking and strength-representing creatures in the wild. The bald eagle is America's mascot. So, locusts, which can come out in swarms of billions and decimate crops, are not a bad animals, but an owl or an eagle (or the bat, which feeds on the locust, katydid, and grasshopper) are? Owls, eagles, kites, and storks eat rats, skinks, chameleons, rabbits, and most of the other animals that are detestable. Is that why these birds are such terrible creatures, because one is what one eats? They are, after all, only eating the animals God created for them to eat.

The edicts of keeping kosher are a God-deemed formality with many humans professing it is a much healthier lifestyle. I will have to disagree, and cite the Asian people. The people of Asia have the most varied diet, and will consider almost anything food; from insects to dogs and cats, seaweed, all manner of fish and fowl, Asian cuisine is diverse. On average, the Asian person lives longer and with less cancer, diseases, and other ailments of other peoples. They certainly do not keep kosher, so that takes the kosher-for-a-healthier-life out of the equation. Back to Noah, and what animals he can save, read below:

Genesis 7:1 The LORD then said to Noah, "Go into the ark, you and your whole family, because I have found you righteous in this generation. Take with you seven of every kind of clean animal, a male and its mate, and two of every kind of unclean animal, a male and its mate, and also seven of every kind of bird, male and female, to keep their various kinds alive throughout the earth. Seven days from now I will send rain on the earth for forty days and forty nights, and I will wipe from the face of the earth every living creature I have made."

I am confused, for if God wanted to wipe clean the earth of all unclean men and animals, why would he have Noah save ones that are unclean? Would they not just breed again one the flood was over? It is a citation that the bible is non-sensible (and did you see and digest the emboldened examples above in the Leviticus verses?). Why not make man a vegetarian? Would not that solve any problem or question of what animals to eat or not eat? Also, why are mushrooms not listed? Mushrooms, after all, feed off of decay. Eating a bottom-feeder or scavenger is not kosher, but eating a mushroom is—that is a faux pas. This also brings us to another very big contradiction on the bible, as found in the book of Timothy.

1 Timothy 4:1 The Spirit clearly says that in later times some will abandon the faith and follow deceiving spirits and things taught by demons. Such teachings come through hypocritical liars, whose consciences have been seared as with a hot iron. They forbid people to marry and order them to abstain from certain foods, which God created to be received with thanksgiving by those who believe and who know the truth. For everything God created is good, and nothing is to be rejected if it is received with thanksgiving, because it is consecrated by the word of God and prayer.

Did Timothy just say that the Spirit (Jesus, ultimately God) forbids people to abstain from eating certain foods? Never mind the whole forbid to marry line where I would think many Catholic priests would be protesting their lot in life, but Timothy clearly says that **everything** created by God is good, and **nothing** is to be rejected. This contradicts every edict in Leviticus, and appears to be saying that God's words (as God Himself mandated all of the kosher edicts) are flat out wrong. This also begs the question, is lent a heretical time of the year? If nothing is to be forbidden, then forbidding meat—especially meat—would make lent heresy. Timothy may explain why [orthodox] Jews are kosher yet Christians are not.

But, you see, it all comes to light when you realize that God is not real, Judaism and Christianity are two fabricated religions (aren't they all?), and that it is simply men trying to control other men. To be painfully redundant, if God were real He would have not made unclean and abominable creatures. If He had, it shows that God is neither perfect nor tolerant, as he either tries to kill them via drowning or protect them via edicts not to eat or even come into contact with them.

"A man can have sex with animals such as sheep, cows, camels and so on. However he should kill the animal after he has his orgasm. He should not sell the meat to the people in his own village, however selling the meat to the next door village should be fine."
Ayatollah Khomeini, 1902 - 1989

"I'm completely in favor of the separation of Church and State. My idea is that these two institutions screw us up enough on their own, so both of them together is certain death."
George Carlin, 1937 –

Sixteen: Potpourri

Before we conclude I would like to add a chapter for some odds and ends, and ask/answer some of the questions I came up while writing this book. Some are my own thoughts, and some are older, already spoken of loose ends that have been asked by great (and free-thinking) minds by famous, infamous, and obscure people.

One of my favorite arguments is that God is supposed to be the only god out there. All other gods are fake, but they exist nonetheless. You would think that God, after He had made Himself known via the Jews, would purge human mythology and history of all traces of these fake gods. That, of course, never happened. I love mythology, especially that of the Norse, and, if you did not know, all of the days of the week are named after Germanic and Norse gods. Why would God allow this, and moreover, NEVER correct it?

- Sunday, or Sunnon-dagaz: named for the sun.
- Monday, Mon, for the moon.
- Tuesday, named for Tyr, Norse God of Justice & War
- Wednesday, named for Woden, King of the Norse Gods
- Thursday, for Thor, son of Odin and God of Lightning
- Friday, for Freya, Norse Goddess of Fertility and of the Valkyries
- Saturday is arguable. Some historians say it is for the Greek god Saturn, others for the Norse fire demon-god Surtur.

Why do the faithful hate the un-faithful? Why do they wish us (or in many cases perpetrate upon us) violence and murder? Are they not breaking their own moral codes? Why are they not heeding the teachings of their respective messiahs? Why are they so concerned about what other people think and believe if they themselves are strong and secure in their own faith? It stands to reason that if Pascal is correct, and all the non-believers are just plain out of luck when they die, why is that not good enough for those who love to hate? Let us be judged, let us burn and suffer, and worry about your own life and dilemmas. Let that woman who had an abortion pay when her time is up. Let the people who were kind and gentle yet did not believe a certain way face their final judgment, and do not perpetrate hate and violence on them while they still live. They cannot. Those who are religious cannot because the mind-virus of religion has corrupted them into to hating everyone who does not think and believe like they do. They cannot because they feel some need to defend an all-powerful being. They cannot because deep down inside humans are animals, and while I have a hard time thinking human nature exists any more, our animal instincts tell us to kill what we fear and what we term different.

Why did God wait all these thousands of years to have His word spread? Why did He choose some back-water people in the middle of the desert to be His chosen people? There were many thousands times more people living in China, India, Europe, the Mediterranean, and South America at that time in history. Why waste time with uneducated (on a worldly scale, that is) people in the middle of the most harsh place on the planet? Why did God not impart his message

109

to cave men who came long before us? Why did the ice ages almost wipe humans from the planet numerous times without divine intervention? We cannot concern ourselves with numbers and relevant equations of mathematics and statistics about the world's population at that time in history when God appears. The bottom line is that if a deity wanted its word spread, it would choose either the most populated region if not <u>all</u> of the population at once.

There is no conceivable point in time and human history when we gave up being hunter-gatherers to take on agriculture and science. To say that God, after waiting about for untold millennia, breathed life, souls, and intelligence into us as a species is ridiculous. Cave men and early modern man had little time for the arts or for recreation. Life was harsh, the climate was killing us, and it took all of man's time to just hunt for food, make clothes and weapons, and find shelter. When we finally managed to figure out that agriculture was the way of the future, we began to smarten up. It is not that modern man is any smarter than early man—we have the same brains as our forefathers from 100,000 years ago. We just have a broader repertoire of knowledge and experience to draw from.

"If God has spoken, why is the world not convinced?"
Percy Bysshe Shelley 1792 – 1822

Wedding vows are a serious matter. Almost all traditional Judeo-Christian-based wedding vows deal with promising before God and/or Jesus Christ to sanctify the marriage. In return, God and/or Jesus promise to make the marriage strong and ever-lasting. "Let no man undo what God has done" is part of a Christian line for wedding vows. If so, why do people of faith get divorced? Did they not swear before God and get a cosmic nod in return? Did God Himself not promise to keep the marriage strong until death parts the lovers? If God gave His word, why would He rescind it (and after you add free will into the picture, it remains the same, for God does not mention free will in wedding vows, and only promises to keep the marriage strong). If God is real and omnipotent, how do you explain the divorce of faithfully religious people? Did you know, statistically speaking, that divorce rates are the lowest among atheist couples, and highest among couples of faith. Check the facts, and do some research. You will find this 100% true.

While we talk of weddings and marriages, why do some sects of Christianity consider divorce a sin? Is it because the vows were made in front of God, and a mortal would be in danger of breaking an oath made to God? If so, what of it when God breaks his oaths as in above, not to mention all the other false promises? Is it better to stay in a horrible, loveless marriage? Is it better to stay with a woman who, for example, treats you horribly and cheats on you? Is it better to stay in a marriage, for example, where a boozing husband constantly beats his wife? Is it a sin for the wife to <u>not</u> want to be beat? Is it not a sin to live in a loveless, terrible marriage where the spouses hate each other and lie? Is that not bearing false witness?

"Now the answer is plain, but it is so unpalatable that most men will not face it. There is no reason for life and life has no meaning. The great tragedy of life is not that men perish, but that they cease to love."
William Somerset Maugham, 1874 - 1965

I recall my college days. I had this professor of economics who was quite an eccentric fellow. Mr. Cronin was an older Irish Catholic who had been through WWII, had a wry sense of humor, and hated women. Man was this guy a misogynist! He was always telling blonde jokes, or women jokes. He talked more about WWII and his nagging, spiteful wife than economics. I know of girls in the class that busted their behinds, worked hard, passed all the tests, and still got grades that deserved a higher mark. Myself and my two buddies, Paul and Dean, were in the same class. Heh—we should have failed. We did not do a darned thing all year, failed a few tests, and never did the homework. We all got B's for a final grade, and I think it was because one day Mr. Cronin's car died, and we pushed it out of its parking space to where Paul's car was and gave it a jump start. It is amazing that, over his career, he was never sued or fired for his hate of women, but this was in the late 1980's, before the other horrible disease of political correctness took over our society.

Anyway, I ramble on because the reason Mr. Cronin had such a hate on women, I suspect, was that he hated his wife. They married, had two sons, but grew apart shortly after. They stayed together despite that they hated each other, and Mr. Cronin filled every class with some stories of Nazi-controlled Europe and tales of how he hated his wife. I still recall his answer when some classmate asked why he did not just get a divorce and move on. His reply? "Oh, no, we couldn't do that. We are good Catholics, and to divorce would be a sin."

Imagine how miserable that household must have been. The real sin was Mr. Cronin and his wife staying together and living in hate.

As it stands, there are over 4,000 types of mammals. Of those 4,000 less than 5% are monogamous creatures, and humans are <u>not</u> on that list. We were not intended to be on that list, at least not by Mother Nature's standards. Male bulls and bears and lions could care less about monogamy. I am sure early man cared little as well, but as our brains grew and a conscience emerged, we could make choices, and monogamy is a choice, not a divinely-inspired way of life.

Why do churches and synagogues have lightning rods, and fire/burglar alarms? That shows an <u>amazing</u> lack of faith, does it not?

To harp more on salvation and sin, as I write my book-long diatribe it dawns on me that all sin and all vice and all "evil" should make no difference to a Christian person. Since we know Christianity is not about ethics or morals and is all about salvation, why does sin even matter? The Catholics love their sins, and cannot get enough of them. Not only sloth, gluttony, and pride and the other four original sins, but being homosexual, masturbation, being too rich, using too many natural resources, talking on the cell phone while driving...where does it end? Each year, or so, the Pope comes up with new sins. Why do they matter? It stands to reason that a person could be an overweight, prideful, rich homosexual who masturbates, and talks on his cell phone while driving his huge SUV that uses too much gas. On top of all that, this person could be a child-molesting, rapist, murderer, and could then just repent to be saved. What this fictional man does in his living years matters not, for he could live an utterly sinful life yet be saved by just admitting his guilt, repenting, and accepting Jesus. That being the case, why does sin matter? Who cares if we sin or not? God could care less, for all you must do is repent those sins and your slate is washed clean.

"How do I define God? I don't... People who find such conceptions important for themselves have every right to frame them as they like. Personally, I don't. That's why you haven't found my "thoughts on this critical question." I have none, because I see no need for them (apart from the - often extremely interesting and revealing -inquiry into human culture and history)."
Noam Chomsky, 1928 -

Does the commandment of thou shall not kill/murder apply to only humans? If you interrupt it as "thou shall not murder", it would make sense. If the word becomes "kill", how would men kill to eat? Theologians have debated this for millennia. My question is this: does it indeed apply to animals? In 5,000 BC when the moral codes were written, men hunted animals for food. Very little sport hunting was going on. Would hunting a tiger, or a boar, or a fish just for the thrill of the kill be breaking the commandment? A fundamentally religious Jew or Christian would not agree, for these people believe that animals are not special, have no souls, and are ours to do with as we please. How do we, and lesser beings when compared to God and the Hosts of Heaven, know this? Up until a hundred years or so ago, mankind walked and/or used pack animals for transportation (not including ships and trains). Cars and trucks were not even a dream of fancy to ancient man, and so death by such means was not an issue. What if a person kills someone unintentionally with a vehicle—is that murder? Is that a punishable offense in the eyes of God? I am not speaking of a drunk driver mind you, but an average, sober motorist.

Why do religious people cry at funerals? It seems like a conflict of religion and reality. If we are all God's creations, and Heaven is to be our destination where we can be with God and all our loved ones, why all the crying? Is this not what people are after all along? Should one not be happy that the deceased is on their way to the pearly gates? Is not crying and wishing the person to still be alive a form of coveting? I can see if the deceased was a horrible, terrible person and it was known he/she was going to hell. That would be reason to cry for them. I suspect people cry because they will miss the person dearly, and that life without them will be a sadder, lonelier place. Then again, if we all lived as I have proposed, death will become a little less painful. It is never easy to lose someone you love and care about. If, however, we step back and look at the bigger picture, we can see the way the departed have touched our lives and made it a better life while they were living.

I see people of good moral character as a benefit to this world and this life—not moral character derived from religion; we have already beaten that horse to death. I find it sad in that, when the world loses a decent, intelligent, giving human, we all lose. I am not going to get into abortion, and I am not going to play the "what if" game. I will say that too many innocent and/or productive people of history have been censored or killed in the name of God. When someone that has benefited society in any way dies I would rather celebrate what they lived for and did while alive rather than mourn too much over their death. Celebrate the good and forget the bad, because the future we can change, but the past we cannot.

Why are other societies not mentioned in the Torah or the bible? There is much ado about the Hittites, Canaanites, Egyptians, and other Assyrian peoples, but never any word of the early Britons, the Saxons, the North and South American Indians, the Inuit in their frozen tundra, the Mongolians, the people of Easter Island, Madagascar, or the Australian Aborigines. We hear nothing of Stonehenge, which we know was built in 2,500 BC, and it was Europe's largest stone-age undertaking. We hear nothing of the Mayans, Incas, Aztecs, and other tribes who had flourishing nations and societies that could rival Egypt at the height of its power. Did God deign to withhold all such information from the desert people of the Nile delta, Persia, and the rest, or is it more likely that these people knew nothing of life outside their desert (and even when Rome came to power did they know of all such foreign lands? We know that is not the case.) Other nations, other people, and other societies are not mentioned because a lack of man's knowledge of the world.

The bible tells us not to kill or murder—people are still debating over the semantics—yet the bible is all about killing and murdering. Most of this death is perpetrated by God, or has mankind perpetrating it because of a command from God. As such, why is suicide a sin? You are using your free will to execute yourself and go to the kingdom of God sooner. God knew you would do this anyway, since He created all there ever was or will be, and knows the hearts of men, so what is the big deal?

On the matter of suicide: if it is a sin, does it matter how long it takes you to commit suicide? If you put a gun to your head in 1934 and pull the trigger in 1984 is that suicide? I suppose so; it just took you fifty years to pull that trigger. You *knew* the gun would fire and end your life. In return you get to burn in Hell. What if you ingested arsenic every day for fifty years, and it eventually killed you? You took a poison knowing it may well kill you, yet you did not stop. Is that suicide? What, then, if you smoked cigarettes for fifty years? You began smoking in 1934 and died of lung cancer and/or emphysema in 1984. You lit all those cigarettes *knowing* it would cause cancer or sickness. It just took fifty years to off yourself instead of putting a gun to your head and blowing your brains out. What if you drank yourself to death because you were an alcoholic? I asked a devout Catholic friend of mine these questions, and he stuck to his guns saying that these two situations are not suicide. He said that you used your free will to smoke and/or drink, and death due to lung cancer or siroccos or alcohol poising would not be suicide. I tried to argue that it was, just that it is slow suicide. I still say I am right, but I am biased to my own opinion.

To expand a tad more on suicide, let us, for argument's sake, say God is real and that suicide is an unforgivable sin. To take your own life is an act that is reprehensible to God, and to do so would mean eternal punishment. If you are killed or murdered, however, that is on the straight and narrow, as long as you are among the faithful. A faithful and fearful person, if killed or murdered, will go directly to Heaven and will be welcomed with open arms. Why then, do humans possess survival instincts? If being killed will get you to Heaven and closer to God, why fight it? Why fight sickness and death? Why fight the rapist who may murder you? Why run from the crazy, chainsaw-wielding maniac? Why battle the lion or bear as it rips you apart? Why is because humans, like all forms of life in this reality, have the survival instinct. We do not want to die. We do not want to go quietly into that dark night. It is greed and lust for life, to stay alive that much longer. It is reasonable to argue that God should have never put survival instincts into humans if we are divine creations. It is reasonable to argue that since we do have survival instincts we are lumped in with all other forms of animals, and that to survive is a natural defense mechanism. Faithful people should not have this defense, then, and since we humans do they should train themselves not to fight or ward off death....or is keeping oneself alive breaking a commandment? Is coveting life not still coveting? Why should we covet our lives if God wants us all to die in the long run so we can sing His praises for eternity in Eden, but be taught some lesson along the way?

Why does the Catholic Church keep inventing new sins? The original seven were not enough? Not only should you not be too proud or too fat, but excessive wealth? The Vatican, in 2007, released seven new sins, and excessive wealth is among them. Is not the Catholic Church one of the world's wealthiest organizations? I have traveled to Rome, and I have visited the Vatican. The amounts of riches lining the areas you can see are staggering. The amount of gold and silver and ivory adorning the halls, walls, decorations, statues, picture frames, and doors could feed the world twice over if sold. The artwork is priceless. I would call all that alone "excessive wealth". Why does the Catholic Church not sell off the art, the precious metals, and, after paying the salaries of the employees, give every penny to non-religious charities, and help feed the world?

"The fact that a believer is happier than a skeptic is no more to the point than that a drunken man is happier than a sober one. The happiness of credulity is a cheap and dangerous quality."
George Bernard Shaw, 1856 - 1950

Other new sins include polluting the environment, birth control, and scientific research that could "offend" God. All rubbish. If we have divinely-given free will, we can do as we please. How would it offend God if He knew what we would do before we do it? It's not about sinning; it is about controlling us and keeping us in line. Sin is an illusion. We make choices, and have to deal with the consequences in this life.

What one calls a sin I call a judgment call. Is it a sin to over-eat and be a glutton? Of course not. It may make you fat and give you diabetes, or you may suffer a heart attack, but it is not a sin. Is it a sin to kill another person? No, but it is a horrible thing to do unless that person is a criminal who is trying to do you harm. Is it a sin to be wealthy? No, for if you spent your hard-earned education and all of your time to chasing your goals to become rich (legally) why not be proud (another non-sin) of your achievement and reap the benefits?

What should be a sin is mandating that [Catholic] priests be celibate. It goes against the very nature of a human male's genetic make up to deny him sexual activity. As I said before there is no more human behavior, only behavior, but in this case our evolved brains still rely on our natural bodies and DNA make up. Males of our species are not naturally monogamous creatures, and we are designed to sew our seeds, to propagate our species. When you deny a male of the desire and ability to have sex, and then make masturbation a sinful act, you set the stage for men to do horrible acts like rape and/or child molestation. We all know that the Catholic Church and its out-dated mandates are ultimately responsible for its clergies' actions. You would think that knowing about such deviant behavior and covering it up would be a sin as well. As much as I admire conviction, it should make anyone stop and wonder why a man would willingly enter into an institution that denies him his basic genetic needs and desires. The argument of being "called by God" is lame if you figure that if God were real, we should all be called to God, free will or not.

The argument above becomes only more evidence that Christianity has nothing to do with morals, and is only about salvation. Were it not, these priests would never sexually molest a child. These priests may go to jail or may one day face their shame, but in their dark hearts they know that all is well and all is good, for all they need to do is take a knee, repent, and all is forgiven.

Sin is not real. Sin is a set of values put in place by the clergy to make you less of a human and more of a slave to religion. There is right and wrong; there is no such thing as good and evil. We humans need to take responsibility for our actions and not use some higher power as a scapegoat or crutch. Good and evil is no more real than Charlie Brown's Great Pumpkin. We either do the right thing or the wrong thing in any given situation. It is the consequences we must deal with since we have evolved higher brain function and have what we call as a conscience. It is always harder to do what is right. One does not need religion to know right from wrong, and it is often religion that is the source of what is wrong.

"I may not be a religious man Reverend, but I know right and I know wrong and I have the good grace to know which is which."
Nicholas Angel, character in the movie *Hot Fuzz*

I always get a chuckle out of those who do dirty deeds, or commit violence and then thank or praise God. Watch a boxing match, or a mixed martial arts match. They are not "dirty", but it is still violence for the sake of violence—but do not get me wrong. I love boxing and MMA, and watch it all the time out of respect for the prowess of the athletes. Quite often you will see the fighters cross themselves and/or take a knee and offer up a quick prayer. Imagine yourself as God as the request comes in. "Dear God, please give me the strength and conviction to beat the living crap out of my opponent. Thank you." Then, after the match, the victor does the same thing, and thanks God and Jesus for giving him the strength and skill to have beaten the crap out of another man. You have to ask, does God get a jolly out of this? Does God enjoy watching people brutalize each other? God obviously likes war and sacrifice, punishment and genocide, so cage fights seem to fit the agenda. Soldiers often beseech God and Jesus for skill to kill and not be killed. A fighter, soldier, or warrior begs and then praises God for his/her years of training and developed skill, skills used to beat or kill another human. Amusing. Mark Twain put it much more elegantly, but what of the prayers of soldiers and their leaders during war. Again, imagine you are God when the beseeching starts. "Oh, Lord, lend me the strength and conviction to kill my enemies, lay low their forces, and wipe my opponents from the face of the Earth. Give me succor as I blow them apart, destroy their cities, and inflict untold suffering. I know they are asking the same of You, but screw them and favor me. Thank you, Lord."

"O Lord our God, help us tear their soldiers to bloody shreds with our shells; help us to cover their smiling fields with the pale forms of their patriot dead; help us to drown the thunder of the guns with the shrieks of their wounded, writhing in pain; help us to lay waste their humble homes with a hurricane of fire; help us to wring the hearts of their unoffending widows with unavailing grief; help us to turn them out roofless with their little children to wander unfriended the wastes of their desolated land in rags and hunger and thirst, sports of the sun flames of summer and the icy winds of winter, broken in spirit, worn with travail, imploring Thee for the refuge of the grave and denied it..."
Mark Twain, 1835 – 1910, *The War Prayer*

Supposing God is real and did create the universe, we humans are special to God. He created the earth for us. God created the whole universe for us. It is all for us! Is that why almost every environment on earth will kill us? Is that why the world is full of animals with claws and fangs and horns to shred us, poison us, give us diseases, and devour us? Is that why slight differentials in air temperature make us ill, or kill us? Is that why most of the world is covered in water that can drown us, or wipe our cities off the map? There are mountains to climb and scale, yet a simple fall from one can crush our bodies to paste (even a short fall can be fatal), not to mention these same mountains can let loose with avalanches, as well as mud and rockslides. There are volcanoes, earthquakes and hurricanes, tornadoes and cyclones, tsunamis and mud slides, droughts, floods, wildfires, and ice ages that last thousands of years. Comets and meteors routinely strike this small, insignificant planet every so often, and some cause extinction-level damage. A simple piece of popcorn or a sucking candy swallowed the wrong way can put us six-feet under. Is all this because one woman ate an apple?

Why is our planet billions and billions of miles away from other uninhabited planets, let alone the countless light years away from any possibly inhabited planets? If the universe was created for us to explore, why would it take hundreds, thousands, or millions of years to reach the "other places" God made for us to explore when we only have but a few decades of life within us? Why does outer space not cater to us? A few seconds in that hostile environment is all it takes to do us in. Why is our sun dying? It will take millions and millions of years, but it is a dying star. Was all this planned that way by a perfect creator?

If you continue this line of thinking, why were we humans not given technology from the beginning of creation? Why were we brought to life in ancient times in but a garden as opposed to thriving metropolises with comforts and conveniences? Instead of an apple tree, Adam and Eve could have been in a tropically-based high-rise penthouse, with a fancy computer that had an apple tree screensaver, and been told not to use the high-speed internet or else all would turn bad and future generations would rue the day. Would not an omniscient deity make us with full knowledge of the universe, and have technology, science, and medicine from the start? If such an omniscient being created us, did it not see that we would one day obtain these achievements any way, and that such medicines and advancements would save countless lives… or is it possible that ancient man, in his ignorance of the world and the universe created the gods to explain all those as-of-yet unexplained questions, phenomena, and ways of the world?

If you study physics, quantum physics, astrology, and locomotion, you will see that space travel is all but impossible, at least as far as a science fiction standpoint. Light speed and warp travel sounds good on the TV or big screen, but ask any qualified physics professor and you get a different answer. Other planets and the stars themselves are outside our reach, and will be for uncountable generations. Even if there were a planet in another galaxy or system that had any sort of life, it would take mankind thousands, even millions of years, to reach even with fictional travel such was war drive. Why? If the universe was made for us to explore, why are not the other planets not populated with God-fearing humans and why are they not within our ability to travel to? Moreover, why even create other worlds in the first place? If God is real, why would He make Mars, Jupiter, Pluto, and the rest? There are untold billions of planets aside from our third rock from the sun. They serve no function in the grand scheme of things. They have no purpose to mankind. They support no life, and do not offer miracles. The stars glow and make the night sky pretty, but why are there other planets if we will never reach them?

There but for the grace of God I go. How many times in your life have you heard or uttered such sentiments? Have you ever thought about that statement? What it says, in other words, is *damn, I'm lucky I'm not that person—thanks, God, for afflicting someone else with that suffering and agony and not me.* As such, why do humans suffer so many birth defects? If we are God's beloved creations (regardless of whether we are born sinners or not) why do so many terrible conditions manifest? Mongoloidism, mental retardation, conjoined twins, palsy, blindness, deafness, and spina bifida are just a few examples of the horrible conditions with which a human can be born. Such cases are rare in the animal kingdom aside from humans. Maybe it is just me, but I have never heard of a mongoloid snake, or a retarded dog or cat. I have never heard of a fish with Down syndrome, or a bird with a cleft beak. Malformations like blindness, deafness, two-headed animals, albinism and other naturally occurring birth defects affect all living things, but it seems we humans suffer the most (and the most severe). Going back to evolution, it seems more to the point that humans are descended from lower life forms, and were are nature's experiment rather than a divine creation.

Why do religious people look down upon the non-religious? Why do they feel that they and they alone know the truth of the universe and that their beliefs make them the moral superior of all other people? Why are the religious—in their eyes—better equipped to do anything? I remember, perhaps seven or so years back, when an American woman gave birth to sextuplets. It made national news. She was interviewed left and right, and asked all the usual questions. When asked if her and her husband were ready for such a challenge, and if they could raise all six children, she replied, "Of course. We are good Christians." So, only a Christian could raise sextuplets? Only Christians are capable parents? What about the rest of us poor shlubs? It makes you want to explode and say that a good <insert religion here> is an oxymoron. In most cases I truly adhere to that.

"During almost fifteen centuries has the legal establishment of Christianity been on trial. What has been its fruits? More or less, in all places, pride and indolence in the clergy; ignorance and servility in the laity; in both, superstition, bigotry, and persecution."
James Madison, 1731 – 1836, 4th President of the United Sates and "Father of the Constitution"

"If I were to mock religious belief as childish, if I were to suggest that worshiping a supernatural deity, convinced that it cares about your welfare, is like worrying about monsters in the closet who find you tasty enough to eat, if I were to describe God as our creation, likening him to a mechanical gorilla, I'd violate the norms of civility and religious correctness. I'd be excoriated as an example of the cynical, liberal elite responsible for America's moral decline. I'd be pitied for my spiritual blindness; some people would try to enlighten and convert me. I'd receive hate mail. Atheists generate about as much sympathy as pedophiles. But, while pedophilia may at least be characterized as a disease, atheism is a choice, a willful rejection of beliefs to which vast majorities of people cling."
Wendy Kaminer, 1950 –

Seventeen: Closing Arguments

What have we learned so far? Aside from the fact that I can be long-winded, like telling anecdotes and bad jokes, can go off on tangents here and there, and am vehemently anti-religion, I hope you, the reader, came away with at least some good out of this book. We have learned that the Old and New Testaments are but books, man-made books crammed with genocide, acts of intolerance, violence, rape, murder, and war. We have learned that religion has held us back more than it has ever propelled us as a species. We have discredited the bible as a source of any true scientific knowledge. I have shown you just a fraction of the discrepancies, contradictions, and falseness that is contained with the pages of the bible.

Now that you are all but done with my rants, you have probably been asking yourself where and how I came up with all of this information. As I have argued, the bible is its own worst enemy, and much is garnered by pouring over it and seeing just what is written. The opinions are my own, but the information, empirical data, and our own world history are out there. Go to a library, read a history book or three, search internet database sites, talk to historical scholars. Nothing in this book is invented or secret knowledge. Like the *X-Files*, the truth is out there. You just have to look for it and take off those blinders.

How does one even begin to defend religion? One thing is for sure and that is religion can never be defended with facts. Religion can never be backed up by empirical data. Religion cannot be defended by reason, with rationality, or with decisiveness. The only defense religion can muster is faith. Faith is not tangible. Faith is not truth. Faith requires blind devotion, the setting aside of one's faculties and reason, and the inflating of one's ego. Faith is that same five-year old with their hands over their ears, eyes shut tight and singing loudly. 'The truth shall set you free' is so on the money that it is scary (if you are of faith, that is). Religion has been backed into a corner by science, technology, and reality. It is doing its best to claw and bite to stay alive, and relies on the gullibility and fears of all that it infects to survive another day, another year. It is not a matter of if Judeo-Christianity will die, but when. All religions will die, as most have. Cults and clubs aside, if humans can stop killing themselves long enough to see the future, ultimately there will be very little religion in it.

People do not need a book, a religion, or the clergy to tell us how to live moral, kind lives. Morals have never come from religion. Morals have come from living together in societies. Morals have come from our cognitive and rational minds, and being able to discern right from wrong, not from religious texts or from the mandates of anthropomorphized gods. Humans are not alone when it comes to morals in that many other animals show signs of morals and values. Elephants, for example, will stay with a dead baby elephants for days, guarding the body, and expressing remorse and loss. Lions will stick together and tend to one another when one is injured and cannot hunt or feed itself, as will wild dogs, hyenas, as well as many herd animals. I grew up on Cape Cod, on a lake. Many a day was it when I awoke to the site of Canadian geese munching the grass of my back yard. Have you ever seen the way Canadian geese eat? When it is just two geese, a male and a female pair, the male will stand by and watch as the female eats. The male will not dip his head once to eat, drink, and will even preen less while she is eating. That seems like pretty moral behavior to me.

Animals, for the most part, are strictly programmed; they are all about survival and in a most selfish way, especially when it comes to food. Go, then, and watch crows eat. I feed the crows in my backyard daily, and when I toss some food for one, it will first find a high branch on which to perch. It will then call, rather raucously, his friends to come and dine. Most animals would race over and scarf down the food before any other beastie could claim it, but the crow will call its mates and let them know food is to be had. Call it a survival tactic, but is that not what "morals" are? Truth is truth, and any society that has decent brainpower can figure right from wrong and not need a religion to dictate this. There is even an amazing viral video out there of two canines in South America crossing a huge highway. One dog is struck by a truck at high speed, and run over. The other dog, risking life and limb—and for no reason other than what was going on in its canine mind—braved the traffic to first stand guard over its friend, and then drag it's fallen buddy to the side of the road as cars and trucks skirted by, nearly killing it as well. You can search the web for the video and watch the amazing display for yourself.

Now, if you believe in the god of Judeo-Christianity, you are taught that animals are just empty shells; sacks of meat, muscle, and bone with no soul and no worth other than food and fodder. This egotistical view places no morals with the minds of animals, leaving goodness solely to humankind. The selfless act of that dog alone testifies that such a narrow, egocentric view is shattered and rendered bankrupt. It may not be human morals, but animals are indeed capable of acts of selflessness. Call it natural selection, hereditary traits for preservation of the species, or say that I am reaching when I say geese, elephants, and canines (and other animals) can show emotion, compassion, and so-called moral behavior, but it shows that kind acts come from nature and natural selection, and not man-made books and morally bankrupt philosophies. If I were to invent a religion, and have it set to words in the form of a book of tenants for its followers, it would be a short, simple book. It would not even be a book; it would be a pamphlet at best. It would read something like this:

Begoodism: How to be a good, moral human being

Treat people as you would like to be treated. Treat people with respect so long as they deserve it. Respect is king!
Do not hate people based on the color of their skin, their personal and religious beliefs, or their nationality. Like and dislike people based upon their actions not their beliefs.
Do not kill another human unless the circumstances are dire, as in self-preservation.
Do not stick your nose into other people's business unless invited to do so; let them worry about the consequences, and do not make them your concern.
Tolerance is a must and hatred is the path to social destruction.
Give to the needy if you can.

Never stop learning, and never be satisfied with what we know versus what we do not.
Let people have whatever sex life they wish so long as it does no harm to you.
Smile often and compliment people every day—even strangers.
Life is short enough. Do not squander it with self-destructive behavior.
Treat nature and the world with respect as this world may belong to us, but it also
belongs to our children and all future generations.
Remember the past, but do not dwell in it. Learn from history so that the same mistakes
are not made over and over.

You get the point. There is not much more to add to those sentiments. I am not a liberal, and I am not a conservative. I am somewhere in the middle. I have some liberal views, and some very harsh views; for instance, I fully support the death penalty, and believe it should be much more prevalent and used much more often than it is, and that harsher, death-involving punishments should be in effect for numerous types of crimes. I believe in a woman's right to choose what to do and what not to do with her body. I eat meat, wear leather and fur, but am against sport and big game hunting. I support digging for oil in every conceivable place we can, but also support wind and solar projects. I support our military, and know that to secure the peace is to be always ready for war. I do not smoke, drink alcohol, or use any drugs, yet I fully support the legalization of prostitution, marijuana, and certain other "drugs" (so long as they are governed and controlled and taxed).

Why would I support such actions? Alcohol is legal, and it certainly is a drug. By legalizing certain substances, as well as prostitution, we will free up millions of spaces in our jails, and our police and law enforcement workers can use their time, efforts, and billions of our tax dollars to hunt down real criminals. Prostitutes are not criminals. If a man or woman wants to pay another for sexual gratification, is that a crime? Do we really need millions of vice police to regulate human sexual behavior? Make the world's oldest trade legal, make the "workers" get licensed (thus having to pay for said license and permits, increasing tax revenue) and have mandatory health screening. I am not saying to make street corners their work place, but look at Amsterdam and parts of Las Vegas as examples. Talk about stimulating the economy, this is a great way. Stimulation for stimulation! If working girls (and men) pay to advertise their services, receive money for their services, and then spend said money it is a step toward economic recovery. Plus their tests must be paid for on their own, and so doctors will receive revenue, as will the government since licenses must be obtained. It may all be baby step, but it is a step nonetheless. Free up the police to catch murders, rapists, pedophiles, terrorists, arsonists, and so on.

All right—enough of my personal views. I digress yet again—sorry about that.

I think this would be the best of all possible worlds if everybody were an atheist or an agnostic
or a humanist -- his or her own particular brand -- but as for compelling people to this,
absolutely not. That would be just as infamous as their imposing Christianity on me. At no time
have I ever said that people should be stripped of their right to the insanity of belief in God. If
they want to practice this kind of irrationality, that's their business. It won't get them anywhere;
it certainly won't make them happier or more compassionate human beings; but if they want to
chew that particular cud. they're welcome to it.
Madalyn Murray O'Hair, 1919 - 1995

To be redundant, is religion a disease, a sickness? The only answer is, 'yes'. It is a psychosis, a viral disease of the mind. It causes delusions, and makes the mind work against rational thought. It instills intolerance and hate, as well as fear in its victims. Religion answers all unanswered questions, and all as-of-yet undiscovered ways in which our universe works with a simple "God did it" instead of "let's find out how and why, as opposed to taking the path of least resistance."

Like all diseases, religion needs a living host. Like all viruses, it needs to reproduce and spread so it can exist. Religion—Judeo-Christianity especially—uses its hosts to pass on the disease so that it can continue to proliferate, and infect as many hosts as possible. This mind virus has evolved, and taken on a life of its own. Is that religious person who is trying to convince and convert you doing it because he or she truly cares about your [supposed] immortal soul, or is it the disease at work, doing its utmost for the host to spread the infection? You have to wonder…

In closing, the truth really will set you free. Perhaps that is why the religious prefer to keep their faith shrouded in mystery, and keep science and learning out of their clandestine, archaic ways—they know the power of truth, and the light that it sheds is not holy, just revealing.

"Religion is the most malevolent of all mind viruses."
Arthur C. Clarke, 1917 – 2008

There is a cure, though, for diseases like religion: the truth. It is indeed a bitter pill to swallow for many, but the truth really shall set you free. Do not be afraid—take the pill. It is free; you do not need a doctor, a prescription, or insurance. A dose or two is all you need, and the side effects are wonderful—less fear, less hatred, less intolerance, more love, more freedom, and a better quality of life.

Be a good person for the sake of being a good person. Do the right thing because it is the right thing to do, and you will be rewarded with real, tangible rewards. Do unto others and make the world a better place while you are here, but do it for the right reasons, and not out of fear of some vain, jealous deity, or some eternal torment. Help your fellow man, be kinder, be gentler, and be more humane. You do not need religion to teach you this—in fact it is near impossible for religion to teach people how to live good, free, kind lives. Just look inside yourself and think with rationality and with reason. If you live in [religious] fear and cannot break those chains, you are beyond help. You will live and die a slave, and in fear. If you can swallow the pill of truth and see the forest through the trees, however small the gap you open is, it is a start. Life is what we make of it. So far we have done a pretty bad job, but the future is wide open. Think kindly, think free, and think well.

When I became convinced that the Universe is natural that all the ghosts and gods are myths,
there entered into my brain, into my soul, into every drop of my blood, the sense, the feeling, the
joy of freedom. The walls of my prison crumbled and fell, the dungeon was flooded with light and
all the bolts, and bars, and manacles became dust. I was no longer a servant, a serf, or a slave.
There was for me no master in the wide world, not even in infinite space. I was free.
Free to think, to express my thoughts
free to live to my own ideal
free to live for myself and those I loved
free to use all my faculties, all my senses

free to spread imagination's wings
free to investigate, to guess and dream and hope
free to judge and determine for myself
free to reject all ignorant and cruel creeds, all the "inspired" books that savages have produced,
and all the barbarous legends of the past
free from popes and priests
free from all the "called" and "set apart"
free from sanctified mistakes and holy lies
free from the fear of eternal pain
free from the winged monsters of night
free from devils, ghosts, and gods
For the first time I was free. There were no prohibited places in all the realms of my thought, no
air, no space, where fancy could not spread her painted wings
no chains for my limbs
no lashes for my back
no fires for my flesh
no master's frown or threat
no following another's steps
no need to bow, or cringe, or crawl, or utter lying words.
I was free. I stood erect and fearlessly, joyously, faced all worlds. And then my heart was filled
with gratitude, with thankfulness, and went out in love to all the heroes, the thinkers who gave
their lives for the liberty of hand and brain
for the freedom of labor and thought
to those who fell on the fierce fields of war, to those who died in dungeons bound with chains
to those who proudly mounted scaffold's stairs
to those whose bones were crushed, whose flesh was scarred and torn
to those by fire consumed
to all the wise, the good, the brave of every land, whose thoughts and deeds have given freedom
to the sons of men.
And I vowed to grasp the torch that they had held, and hold it high, that light might conquer
darkness still.
Robert Green Ingersoll, 1833 – 1899

Printed in Great Britain
by Amazon